Numbers R Simple

People Are Complicated.

- Learn Astro and Solar Numerology
- How Your Day of Birth Influences You
- Numbers and Their Meanings
- How Numbers Are Simple Relationship Chronicles
- And More!

King Simon

Numbers R Simple

P.O Box 501274

Indianapolis, Indiana 46250

Copyright 2015

ISBN 1517061636

A Charles' Child Production

Melanie D. Stevenson

Cover Design

Melanie D. Stevenson

Marlon W. Stevenson

Numbers R Simple

Numbers R Simple

Disclaimer

The author disclaims any liability caused by the direct or indirect use or misuse of the information in this book. None of the information is meant to take the place of an accredited license medical health practitioner.

Manufactured and Printed in the United States of America

Numbers R Simple

Table of Contents:

CHAPTER 1 7

ASTRO & SOLAR NUMEROLOGY...7

   Astro-Numerology 8

   Solar-Numerology 9

CHAPTER 2 11

FEMININE & MASCULINE NUMBERS 11

Numerical Chart with Gender and Elements 16

Pythagorean Number Chart 17

OTHER NUMBER CHARTS TO USE......................................21

CHAPTER 3 25

YOUR DAY OF BIRTH INFLUENCES YOU 25

CHAPTER 4 31

NUMBERS AND THEIR SIMPLE & COMPLICATED MEANINGS .31

Etymology 34

CHAPTER 5 45

MASTER NUMBERS...45

CHAPTER 6 53

COMPOUND / COMPOSITE NUMBERS (10 – 31) 53

CHAPTER 7 60

NUMBERS CONNECTION TO HEALTH, NAMES & WORDS.......60

CHAPTER 8 69

Numbers R Simple Relationship Chronicles 69

Epilogue 111

Index...114

ACKNOWLEDGMENTS:

Love and honor to the Divine Universal Creative Force (The All) and to all my Ancestors.

- **My late Grandmothers: Lillian Alberta Walters** and **Rachel Robinson.** Thanks for your guidance.
- **To my late Grandfathers: Clifford Hamilton (Papa)** and **Granville 'Sticky' Risden.** I love your essence and strength.
- **To my Mother:** *Earline Brown* for your love, endurance, strength, nurturing spirit and protection from the day I came through you to this realm.
- **To my Father:** *Trevor Brown* for your love, and promotional talents you gave me unknowingly through your connection with my mother.
- **To my talented sister:** *Nicole Brown* thanks for your love, inspiration and faith in me and the Creator.
- **To my Great Children and Grand Children: Adam, Sha-Yah, Jaleel, Khalfani, Ashley, Bryanna, Tariq, Yasira, Jordan, grandchildren Amiyr & Isaiah, their siblings and any other children that may come in the future.** Thank you all for your love and respect and always being willing to learn. Remember, Stay focused— you are always in my meditations & prayers.
- **Love & Respect to the wonderful mothers of my children:** Tasliym, Valda, Marcia, Sharon, Aurelia and Janelle and their extended families. I love and care about you all and you all have done an outstanding job.
- **To my other siblings and their extended families:** Carlos, Katana, Dwayne, Daniel and Leah—I love and respect you all.
- **To my wonderful Aunts and strong Uncles thanks for your love and guidance.**
- **To my cousins on my mother's and father's side thanks for being the wind under my wings for many years. I love you all.**
- **Special Thanks to those who inspired me to do what I love: Lloyd Strayhorn**, James Dillerhunt, Aton Edwards & Family, Abundance Child & Family, **Nysut: Amun-Re Sen Atum-Re (Brother Polight and Family),** Dr. Phil Valentine, Dr. Sebi, Dr. Afrika, Mother Maa, Dr. Ben, **Queen Afua**, Taj Tarik Bey, Sister R.V. Bey, Brother Anpu, The Honorable Elijah Muhammad, The late Father Clarence 13X, Dr. Malachi K. York, and **Natosha 'The Number Swami' McCray**.
- **To those I have not mentioned...Thanks for your inspirational words and continual encouragement into knowledge of self through our ancient lessons and sciences of life.**

I SINCERELY LOVE & RESPECT YOU ALL

Numbers R Simple

FOREWORD 1

By Lloyd Strayhorn

Numbers R Simple . . . People are Complicated

Truer words by King Simon were never spoken when it comes to the title of this book that you are about to explore. He is absolutely right! Numbers are simple. On the other hand, my long experience being in this metaphysical field is that it is PEOPLE that are really complicated. This book is chock-full of useful, practical information that can be applied at a moment's notice, numerically speaking. That in itself is of great value. Where TIME is of the essence when important decisions have to be made—about being in the right place at the right time! In essence, this book is a wonderful guide as to when to do things and GET RESULTS. So, I couldn't agree with King Simon more.

Numbers R simple. However, people are VERY complicated.

Lloyd Strayhorn

Mr. Strayhorn has made numerous television appearances on such shows as "The Oprah Winfrey Show," "Tony Brown's Journal," and "Geraldo." In addition, Mr. Strayhorn has appeared on countless cable TV and radio shows across the country.

www.numbersandyou.com or www.lloyd-strayhorn.com

FOREWORD 2

By ~ Natosha 'The Number Swami' McCray

It's my pleasure to write an introduction to *'Numbers 'R' Simple...*
People are Complicated.'

King Simon is relentless in his pursuit to inform the masses
through his promotions and they have greatly enhanced my life. I
got my first taste of numerology when he brought Lloyd Strayhorn
to events at Nicholas Books. As a result he is a direct link for my
passion for the numbers.

As the Number Swami I am all about those numbers. This book
will be a guiding post for your most peculiar relationships. How
does a 4 connect with a 6, and why we are not the same? You will
have an informative and empowered read. We have to learn how
to connect with one another and use our relationships in a way
that is beneficial for all parties. The numbers will be the language
and King Simon will be the code breaker.

King Simon has been on his numbers games for a minute so don't
sleep on skills. I recommend highly that you engage him and
elevate him in his spiritual evolution because he is about to shift
the game.

This will be one of those books in my library for reference and
actual usage. So enjoy the read, take the journey through
numbers and people.

Peace

Natosha 'The Number Swami' McCray

"Your Dreams Are Our Inspiration To Educate, Empower, and
Inform."

www.TheNumberSwami.com

Check out my blog @ myblog.thenumberswami.com

Numbers R Simple

INTRODUCTION

"Numerology is a do-it-yourself science to help us learn more about ourselves and others." ~ Anonymous

Everything seems to be numbered. We all have become numbers in this world. We even equate various things to numbers like: days, months, the time we were born, etc. From the very first time we picked up a utensil to eat—there is a number attached. Also, our **Birth Certificate, Social Security, Marriage & Divorce Certificates, Death Certificate, Health Records,** etc. all have numbers to keep count of people and their where-a-bouts, transactions and things you may like and dislike daily.

Many of us don't even pay attention to the use of numbers and its importance since the beginning of time. However, numbers are a very important part of our lives and it is here to stay.

As you can see in history numbers have been an intricate part of our lives. The human body (itself) is living mathematics. Like sister *Narubi Selah* says on her album, **'I AM LIVING MATH.'** The body is a three dimensional existence with length and width—which is mathematical and connected to numbers. ***The Most Hon. Elijah Muhammad*** and many of our ancient ancestors have always taught us about the great lesson of mathematics and its connection to humans and life in general.

In this writing we will examine *(through experience)* the simplicity of numbers and how the person or persons connected to the numbers are complicated through various life encounters—from social issues, health issues, family issues and past issues that have affected their present and future lives.

****

Here are brief meanings of the words Number, Simple, People and Complicated. ***According to the Oxford American Desk Dictionary and Thesaurus Second Edition - 2001:***

Number ~ *num•ber* /number/ *•n.* *1* *a arithmetical value representing a particular quantity and used in counting and calculating.* *b word, symbol, or figure representing this; numeral.* ***(Let's go directly to the fifth meaning of the word)*** *5 a person or thing having a place in a series, esp. a single issue of a magazine, an item in a program, etc.*

Simple ~ *sim•ple* /simpel/ *adj.* *1 easily understood or done.* *2 not complicated or elaborate; without luxury or sophistication.*

People ~ /pe`epel/ *• n.[usu. As pl.] 1 a persons composing a community, tribe, race, nation, etc.* ***(Let's go directly to the third & fourth meanings of the word)*** *3 parents or other relatives. 4 subjects, armed followers, congregation, etc.*

Complicated ~ *from the word complicate /komplikayt/ v. 1 make difficult or complex. 2 (as **complicated** adj.) complex.*

****

Numbers R Simple...People are Complicated is just what it says—straight to the point with no chaser. After ten or more years of studying myself and others through numbers it has dawned on me that numbers or numerology is not the blame but it is the choices we make when we don't learn how to chart ourselves. Now, to gain a true meaning and understanding of what it is to know one's self we have to learn how to use these ancient sciences that's been hidden and forbidden from us for so many thousands of years due to dogmatic religions or just those who wanted to keep us under their control. *Astronomy, Astrology, Numerology* and other ancient knowledge and wisdom have been demonized, called occultism, and other crazy labels to mislead the masses from using these ancient ways to obtain a true knowledge of self. Our ancestors knew this would be the case that is why they passed it down through various methods like: *word of mouth, writing it in stone, burying it or engrained in our blood-line (called DNA).* **Whatever the case may be other recordings of OUR story have been made into a "MYSTERY" when it is really "MY-STORY" or OUR STORY.**

I hope you will learn and build upon what I am going to share with you. Knowledge is everlasting and this is just another part of the puzzle being presented in this book called, *'Numbers 'R' Simple...People are Complicated.'* Enjoy! ~ **King Simon Kweku (T.A.B.)**

CHAPTER 1

"Numerology uses numbers as a key to human behavior. It is an easy-to-learn method that exercises the mind's intuitive faculty to fathom the depth of human personality."
~ Harish Johari

ASTRO & SOLAR NUMEROLOGY

The laws that govern us have been proven over and over again by our everyday observance of nature. The Universe is in a constant state of creative law and order. I've met many who say, *"I don't believe in **Astronomy, Astrology, Astro & Solar Numerology, etc.**"* and I always reply, *"You don't have to believe in it— but rest assure that the macro-cosmic universe and all its sciences are connected to you the micro-cosmic universe."* I don't know why many of us can't see the correlation. We are all energy and we are all connected. Our ancient ancestors knew this and if we would research and study for ourselves we would also have this understanding.

In this chapter we will basically deals with a brief break down of *Astro-Numerology* and *Solar-Numerology*. One thing I love to do is show respect to people who deserve it. There are two great brothers I have had the privilege of working with for some time, *Brother Lloyd Strayhorn (whom I've learned from for over 15 years) and Brother POLIGHT (whom I've known since 2009).* I have learned through research and experience that our ancient knowledge of *Astronomy, Astrology, Alchemy, Numerology* and other sciences has been taken from us through reconstructive history and other methods. In this part of the book we are going to simply discuss it by quoting **Lloyd Strayhorn and Brother POLIGHT.**

****

Numbers R Simple...People are Complicated Tip A:

The best way to get full awareness of your potential is to study these proceeding sciences and their counterparts.

****

Astro-Numerology

Astro-Numerology is the study of astrology and its connection to numbers. They are very much related to each other and there are similarities between your astrological graph in connection to your numerological chart in your birth day and name. Also, in Astrology *(or Astro-logics)* there are elements attached to the zodiac such as **Air, Water, Earth and Fire** signs—these elements are also connected to each number from **1 to 9**.

Now, according to **Lloyd Strayhorn's book, 'Numbers and You,' (on page 83)** he states, *"...we're all born under a Sun sign, which denotes one individuality and ego. In Numerology, the Expression number (the sum total of your name at birth) is the equivalent of your Sun sign."*

The Moon in your chart denotes your inner personality, dreams, goals, and desires. In Numerology this is equivalent to the Motivation Number—your heart's desire or soul urge—which is derived from the sum total of the vowels in your name.

Another important factor in Astrology is your ascendant, or rising sign. It denotes the impression you make on others. It also gives clues to your physical appearance. Numerologically, this information is given in the sum total of the consonants in your name, and is known as the Appearance, or Quiescent, number." **For more info, please refer to Lloyd Strayhorn's book, 'Numbers and You.' (numbersandyou.com)**

Solar-Numerology

According to Nysut: Amun Re Sen Atum Re's (Brother POLIGHT) book called, **Solar Numerology: Past Life Exegesis and Divulgence into Your Future on page 204 the Definition of:**

*"**Solar numerology** actually deals with the evaluation of arithmetic so that we may arrive at mathematical interpretations of numbers that represent the nature of people. This means that we have studied how numbers behave in real live mathematical scenarios and then we interpret the behavior of these numbers and relate them to people's nature. Couple this information with the conventional zodiacal approach and you will have solar-numerology. **Solar numerology** represents the summation of your mentality and per-**sun**ality."*

Although there are similarities between Astro-Numerology and Solar-Numerology—the difference is the **Astro (as in Astrology)** and **Solar (as in Solar Biology).**

According to Nysut: Amun Re Sen Atum Re, he states, **"Astrology is the perverted science of our way of life.**

What lunar astrology attempts to accomplish can only be truly resolved by Solar Biology.” He continues by saying that, “the first Solar Biologist was Menes of the first Egiptian Dynasty. Menes was also known in other religions as Enoch, Idris, and Adafa.”

For more info please refer to Brother POLIGHT's book on 'Solar Numerology,' mentioned above. ☺

CHAPTER 2

"The Creator always speaks twice—through stars and numbers."

~ Florence Evylinn Campbell

FEMININE & MASCULINE NUMBERS

I love numbers, the symbol, the word, its ancient origins and its connection to people and our everyday lives. We are all numbered even if we believe it or not.

I remember, studying ancient languages when I was younger and learning that there was a numerical value to various letters, words and even scriptures. Then I found out that each letter and number has a *feminine and masculine* counterpart. How amazing was that to a young person like myself, at the time, on the journey to acquiring more knowledge, wisdom, and understanding. There is an old Buddhist saying that, ***"when the student is ready, the teacher will appear."*** Well, I have never looked back when it comes to studying and learning from those teachers. I am forever a student.

Below are the numbers and their masculine & feminine counterparts:

The Chart

1 Masculine	6 Feminine
2 Feminine	7 Masculine
3 Masculine	8 Feminine
4 Feminine	9 Masculine
5 Masculine	0 Feminine

Note: 0 (Zero) is not considered a number according to European Science because they know that all numbers came from the zero (or the womb).

Also, according to online voters statistic (Yahoo! Answers), **"ZERO IS NOT CONSIDERED AS A FINITE NUMBER BECAUSE A NUMBER THAT HAS ZERO AS THE DENOMINATOR IS UNDEFINED. IN OTHER WORDS, IT IS INFINITE."**

In this section we will cover the *feminine and masculine* meanings of numbers and how it affects or connects with people.

Have you ever wondered—*why some people act more feminine or masculine than others?*

Why some people have more masculine or feminine energies, tendencies or traits than others?

Well, many people have their own explanation but, I have recognized over my years of research that most people you know or find with these tendencies may have multiple amount of numbers in their charts that may sway them towards the masculine or feminine energy. Even when you examine chromosomes—the **number** of chromosomes may tilt towards the feminine in a male or masculine in a female.

The following information is from 'Genetic Kiss' by Paa Munzul Nazdur (Actual Fact #109 page 6-7 * #87 - #105) (For research purposes only)

"...87. Chromosomes are microscopic bodies found in cells during division.

*88. You received 23 chromosomes from your mother and 23 chromosomes from your father giving you 46 chromosomes; different species have a different **number** of chromosomes.*

89. Some have 47 and others have 48.

90. Humans that have 47 chromosomes that have an extra **Y** *chromosome usually occur with males.*

91.Some names for this are **Jacob's Syndrome, XYY Karyotype, XYY Syndrome and YY Syndrome.**

92. With this unbalanced **number** *of chromosomes, they have an extra* **Y** *chromosome in each of their body cells.*

93. In another case they will carry this extra **Y** *chromosome in only some of their cells called* **mosaicism.**

For more regarding the previous info please refer to 'Genetic Kiss' by Paa Munzul Nazdur (Actual Fact #109 page 6-7 * #87 - #105) or do your own research. Below is more info pertaining to the subject.

The following report about Chromosome Imbalances is from www.genomicseducation.ca:

"A chromosome imbalance is when there is extra or missing chromosome material. Differences in the amount of chromosome material affect an individual's growth and development and may cause birth defects and/or mental retardation. Chromosomes imbalances may occur because of a change in the **number** *or structure of the chromosomes."*

Changes in the **number** *of chromosomes*

Usually a person has two copies (disomy) of every chromosome in their body cells.

Trisomy:

- *A Trisomy is when there are three copies of a chromosome instead of two copies.*

- *Often, having a complete chromosome Trisomy is not compatible with life*
- *One exception is Down syndrome. Individuals with Down syndrome are trisomic for chromosome 21. They have three copies of chromosome 21 instead of two copies.*
- *A second exception is individuals with sex chromosome trisomies. For example XXX, XXY, XYY. These individuals are usually healthy, they usually have normal intelligence, and they may have some learning difficulties and fertility problems."*

The same study continues to say:

How do chromosome imbalances happen?

*In the process of making egg and sperm cells, chromosome pairs must separate so that each egg or sperm cell only receives 23 chromosomes. Sometimes this does not happen properly and an egg or sperm cell is made with an extra or missing chromosome. The process by which this failure occurs is called **non-disjunction**.*

If you would like to learn more about the previous study please go to the website *www.genomicseducation.ca.*

(This is for research purposes only)

****

One may ask, "What determines a number and its connection to the feminine or masculine energy? To keep it simple— Universally, there is a balance of the feminine and the masculine or what we in this realm identify with as female and male (Yin & Yang, etc.)—dating far back to Pythagoras and even further than him who received his information from the ancient scribes of Kemet (Egypt). ***Please refer to 'Stolen Legacy' by Professor George G. M. James—*** and other scholars to realize that numbers are as old as dirt.

Numerical Chart with Gender and Elements
M = MASCULINE AND F = FEMININE

1 – M - FIRE

2 – F - WATER

3 – M - FIRE

4 – F - AIR

5 – M - AIR

6 – F - EARTH

7 – M - WATER

8 – F - EARTH

9 – M - FIRE

0 – F – ETHER/VOID

****

Now, in regards to masculine and feminine numbers— your is not the only numbers that may affect you. The numbers associated with your name can bring significant effect to your personality. We will be dealing with the **Expression** numbers in a known celebrity's name and also with his birthday to identify the masculine and feminine connection. We will be using the Pythagorean number chart.

Pythagorean Number Chart

Pythagorean System								
1	2	3	4	5	6	7	8	9
A	B	C	D	E	F	G	H	I
J	K	L	M	N	O	P	Q	R
S	T	U	V	W	X	Y	Z	

Note: The ***Expression*** *number in your name is found by adding all the numbers in your name together. The* ***Motivation*** *number in your name is found by adding all the vowels* **(A, E, I, O, U and sometimes Y)** *together. The* ***Personality*** *number in your name is found by adding all the consonants in your name together.*

Let's take the Rock (**Dwayne Douglas Johnson**) for example:

Dwayne: 4+5+1+7+5+5=27 (9) M

Douglas: 4+6+3+7+3+1+1=25 (7) M

Johnson: 1+6+8+5+1+6+5=32 (5) M

When we add up the results you get the

Expression # 3 (9+7+5=21 and 2+1=3) M

Let's examine his **(the Rock's)** birthday below: **May 2, 1972**

May 2 (Feminine), 1972

5+2+1+9+7+2 = 26 ~ 2+6 = 8 (Feminine)

(Rock) 9+6+3+2 = 20 ~ 2+0 = 2 (Feminine)

Please notice: *Dwayne Douglas Johnson's (The Rock) masculine numbers in his birth name and the feminine numbers and how it is pronounced in his birth-date, life path and the nick name (Rock) he is known by in his career.*

FYI: *The personality number is the actual birthday (May 2nd ~ the 2 is the personality number) and the life path is found by adding the month, day and the year the person was born. Like the above example: 5/2/1972 (5+2+1+9+7+2=26 2+6=8)*

Note: The above use of The Rock's name is to show the reader that the names you choose outside of your birth name can also make a serious energy shift towards the positive or the negative.

My review: *This shows me that his masculine numbers (from his birth names) and his feminine numbers from his birthday (personality and life path) helped to balance his accomplishments in life. Without doubt he has used his* *strong masculine image with his emotional executive energies to galvanize success during his career. (From wrestling to acting)*

****

Numbers R Simple…People are Complicated Tip B:

Study the numbers connected to the name and it will give a birds-eye-view of yourself and other individuals.

The reader can use the number charts below to learn more about their name and birthday and even the names and birthdays of others.

*The proceeding chart is based off of the **Pythagorean Number values**.*

Pythagorean System								
1	**2**	**3**	**4**	**5**	**6**	**7**	**8**	**9**
A	B	C	D	E	F	G	H	I
J	K	L	M	N	O	P	Q	R
S	T	U	V	W	X	Y	Z	

Take myself for example: *Every first name I have used over the years has unknowingly added up to the #7 (according to the Pythagorean System) and when I started studying numerology I found that very interesting.*

ANTHONY: 1+5+2+8+6+5+7= 34 (3+4=7)

S IMON: 1+9+4+6+5= 25 (2+5=7)

Since I don't believe in coincidences—it has shown me how we are connected to numbers and how we can vibrate towards a certain number without even knowing that we are or have been connected to the number since birth.

According to a presentation I heard with Brother Polight, he said, *"that a woman's numerical frequency can change with child birth."* Let's say if a woman is born on **October 24** and she gives birth to her child on **July 31**—then the mother's numerical frequency can slightly change to the number of the child due to childbirth.

Let's examine this couple and their child:

If the mother's birth date is **October 24th (6)** and the father is **August 10th (1)** usually, that couple would have a shaky and challenging relationship. The **#6 (Earth)** is in opposition to **#1 (Fire)** but if the child is born on **July 31st (#4 Air)** then the mother will take on some of that numerical frequency of the child and become somewhat compatible to the father. Both #1 (Fire) and #4 (Air) can work in harmony if both parents understand the value of *pre-planning* or *pre-charting* the child's birth. So, in actuality the child can help with the harmony of the relationship if it is already shaky from the start. Bringing children into the world is a beautiful experience but, in this society many of us don't realize the importance of it and why it should be planned. That is why I mention **charting** and knowing your **ancestry** in my first book, **'No Promotion Is Bad Promotion,' in Chap**. 7.

Note: *Planning Birth is different than Controlling Birth.* That is why **"Planned Parenthood"** was created— not to **PLAN it** but to **CONTROL it** through **Eugenics.** Margaret Sanger a proponent of that science founded it. Please research this for yourself.

OTHER NUMBER CHARTS TO USE

The following number chart was passed down from the elders in Lagos, Nigeria (In Africa) to Ife Maijeh, author of *'The Oracle of Dreams.'*

1 2 3 4 5 6 7 8 9 0

A B C D E F G H I J

K L M N O P Q R S T

U V W X Y Z

Note: We might use the above chart in this book on various occasions to get the point across. The chart was added to make the readers aware that a chart with zero was passed down by elders in Africa according to said author.

The following chart is the Chaldean approach to numerology and is considered an ancient and accurate system. According to history, the people of Chaldea occupied the south part of Babylonia and studied the

occult sciences. They were also known for their contributions to Astronomy, Mathematics, Astrology and Numerology. You may notice that no alphabet or letter was assigned to the number 9. The number 9 was taken out because the Chaldeans believed that 9 was so holy and sacred it was to be held separately from the other numbers.

Chaldean System							
1	2	3	4	5	6	7	8
A	B	C	D	E	U	O	F
I	K	G	M	H	V	Z	P
J	R	L	T	N	W		
Q		S		X			
Y							

For example let use the above Chaldean chart for the name:

TONY ~ 4+7+5+1 = 17 (1+7 = 8)

Refer to the Pythagorean chart:

TONY ~ 2+6+5+7 = 20 (2+0 = 2)

Refer to the Afrikan (Nigerian) chart:

TONY ~ 0+5+4+5 = 14 (1+4 = 5)

According to Lloyd Strayhorn author of, 'NUMBERS AND YOU,' he states on page 12:

"There are many different systems of Numerology. There's an African, an Arabian, and a Hebrew system of numbers. There's the Abracadabra system, which uses the pyramid technique. There's even a system of Japanese Numerology.

The Numerology systems commonly used here in the West are the Pythagorean and Chaldean methods. Of the two, the Pythagorean system is the more popular and easier to use. This explains why one numerologist may tell you your name or birth number is a 7, while another will say that you're a 3. The question to bear in mind is what system was used to arrive at your key number or numbers, and what do they mean?

Both the Pythagorean and Chaldean systems are similar in some respects, yet they have fundamental differences. On the similar side, both systems take your name and month, day and year in which you were born into consideration. Both agree that people's names affect their character, and the birth date affects their destiny. Both systems are equally good in their own way at giving advice. Finally, numbers in both systems carry the same meaning, quality, character, and nature—this seems to be universal under all the systems."

For more information about Astro-Numerologist Lloyd Strayhorn ~ go to www.numbersandyou.com or www.Lloyd-strayhorn.com

FYI: Below is the Five Percent (Nation of Gods and Earths) system of numbers called, **'The Daily Mathematics'** (Based on the teachings of the Hon. Elijah Muhammad):

JUST FOR RESEARCH PURPOSES ONLY.

1. **Knowledge**
2. **Wisdom**
3. **Understanding**
4. **Culture or Freedom**
5. **Power or Refinement**
6. **Equality**
7. **God**
8. **Build or Destroy**
9. **Born**
0. **Knowledge Add on Cipher**

Note: If you need more details regarding 'The Daily Mathematics' please refer to 'Supreme Lessons of the Gods and Earths.

CHAPTER 3

"The two greatest days in your life are; the day you were born and the day you find out why you were born." ~ Les Brown

YOUR DAY OF BIRTH INFLUENCES YOU

The day you were born has a great influence on you and the people around you. As a matter of fact each day is influenced by the number it is associated to, the planet and elements. In various cultures the days were so important that they named their children after the day the child was born. For instance, I was born on Wednesday, so in my ancestry, my name would be **'KWEKU,' son or boy born on Wednesday and this day is ruled by Mercury (#5 ~ Air)** which makes me *quick wit, adaptable and able to respond to emergency conditions.* Now, knowing this bit of information helped me to move accordingly. So, it is not a coincidence that I am a disaster preparedness instructor for over 15 years. When it was introduced to me in the 90s—it just clicked and I used it to my benefit. Find out what day you were born—

via your parents, grandparents, living relatives, etc. or you can refer to **The Perpetual Calendar in Lloyd Strayhorn's book, 'Numbers and You.'**

DAYS, NUMBERS & PLANETS

SUNDAY = 1 & 4 (SUN)

MONDAY = 2 & 7 (MOON)

TUESDAY = 9 (MARS)

WEDNESDAY = 5 (MERCURY)

THURSDAY = 3 (JUPITER)

FRIDAY = 6 (VENUS)

SATURDAY = 8 (SATURN)

Here are simple meanings to day of birth influences:

Sunday ~ can be bright, out-going and happy with great leadership & organizing abilities.

Monday ~ can be very emotional, perceptive and somewhat of a dreamer. If you use your great imagination you can accomplish wonderful things.

Tuesday ~ can be forceful, active and full of energy but should avoid overly heated arguments and learn to cultivate strong willpower.

Wednesday ~ can be fast thinking, curious, freedom loving and possess great resourcefulness. Learn to focus and do one thing at a time and don't over indulge.

Thursday ~ can be very ambitious, goal orientated, have a youthful personality and out-look on life. However, stay away from too much excess and extreme behavior.

Friday ~ can be very loving, caring, and beautiful. Always seek balance in all and give intuitive advice to all who ask for it sincerely.

Saturday ~ can be a little miserable but maintain a mature way of thinking about life and your situation. Stay positive, impartial and you will accomplish great things in life.

Here are simple meanings to Planetary influences:

SUN: Self-expression and personality.

MOON: Habits, moods, emotions, ways and means.

MERCURY: Intellectual ties, communication and opinions.

VENUS: True affection, unity, finances, consideration of partner and partnership.

MARS: Sex life, action and the more aggressive aspects, tiffs and quarrels.

JUPITER: Sense of humor, abundance, shared fun.

SATURN: Constructive progress, karma, but also frustration, ambition, unhappiness; even misery, coldness and frigidity.

URANUS: Originality, the dynamic aspects, the unexpected and general tension.

NEPTUNE: Inspiration, dreamy, idealism, romance, escapism or deception and underhandedness.

PLUTO: Ability to make new beginnings, transformation & destruction, forget the past, and start again.

****

Numbers R Simple...People are Complicated Tip C:

Find out the day of the week you were born and learn about the planets in your chart because it will give you clearer guidance.

THE MONTHS AND THE NUMBERS CONNECTED TO THEM:

January:	1	**July:**	7
February:	2	**August:**	8
March:	3	**September:**	9
April:	4	**October:**	10
May:	5	**November:**	11
June:	6	**December:**	12

Reminder: On how to find out the birth number of a person born on:

February 3, 1964

Month   **February**

2

Day   3
3

Year   1964 (1+9+6+4)
        20

Total
        25

To get to the single digit add 2 + 5 = 7 and that would be the birth number.

Note: The previous information also depends on your zodiac and numerical charts that will add positive or negative results to the day you were born. Please seek advice from a reputable Astrologist, Numerologist and Reader.

****

The following is to briefly inform the readers that numbers are connected to your Astrological signs and your days also—which can determine how it affects you and others around you. So, please make a note of it.

ARIES (MARCH 21-APRIL 20) is connected to **9** and Tuesday.

TAURUS (APRIL 21-MAY 20) is connected to **6** and Friday.

GEMINI (MAY 21-JUNE 20) is connected to **5** and Wednesday.

CANCER (JUNE 21-JULY 20) is connected to **2, 7** and Monday.

LEO (JULY 21-AUGUST 20) is connected to **1, 4** and Sunday.

VIRGO (AUGUST 21-SEPTEMBER 20) is connected to **5** and Wednesday.

LIBRA (SEPTEMBER 21-OCTOBER 20) is connected to **6** and Friday.

SCORPIO (OCTOBER 21-NOVEMBER 21) is connected to **9** and Tuesday.

SAGITTARIUS (NOVEMBER 22-DECEMBER 21) is connected to **3** and Thursday.

CAPRICORN (DECEMBER 22-JANUARY 20) is connected to **8** and Saturday.

AQUARIUS (JANUARY 21-FEBRUARY 19) is connected to **4, 1** and Sunday.

PISCES (FEBRUARY 20-MARCH 20) is connected to **3** and Thursday.

Note: If you notice some dates are not the same as you may know them—remember sign can change due to time zones and places people were born. If you would like to find a more ancient Astro-logics chart please do your research or you can refer to the resources in the back of this book for more information and guidance. ☺

CHAPTER 4

"Alone, neither your stars nor your numbers tell the whole story about yourself, but each one opens the door of the other to fuller understanding and enlightenment."

~ Florence Evylinn Campbell

NUMBERS AND THEIR SIMPLE & COMPLICATED MEANINGS
0 Zero

The State of Mind / Extreme Messenger

The *simplicity* of those born connected to the zero (0). Zero (0) is everything but nothing at the same time. The **zero (0)** is infinite and all numbers came out of it. It is a limitless symbol and those who possess it have great *potential* and *possibilities* if they remain focused and if they have people around them as a higher and positive guidance.

The *complications* of those born connected to the zero like: those born on the **10th, 20th** and **30th** seem to vary from one extreme to the next. They can go through many cycles of life that can lead them into a *constructive or destructive* way of life. Those connected to the **zero (0)** must be guided from young… to the highest and wisest vibration of their leading number. *(1, 2, or 3)*

Interestingly, many would say that zero **(0)** is not a *"number"* on the chart. It is considered a ***universal state***, or in some schools of thought it is a ***state of mind*** or it doesn't **"exist."** But, when added to the numerical chart it would balance the feminine and masculine aspect of said chart. Then it is no coincidence that in computer language **(the binary code)** that the 0 and 1 is dominant and represent a letter, digit, or other character. **One (1 = masculine)** and **Zero (0 = feminine)** must be a balance to maintain the binary code.

The symbol of zero **(0)** is similar to the symbol of the circle **(O)** and in history the circle has been considered the symbol of the universe for thousands of years. The universe has been referred to as feminine by known scientists, scholars and wise men & women for eons. In my humble analysis the zero **(0)** or circle is the symbol on the numerical chart that completes and balances it.

Note: *Just because European scholars and scientists decided to remove the zero (0) from the number chart doesn't mean that it is valid. They have taught us **HIS - STORY** for years and we have to stop letting them dictate what is from what isn't for us.*

****

According to **Harish Johari, author of 'Numerology: A Key to Human Behavior'** he states: *"All numbers from 1 to 9 are present in zero, and when zero combines with these* *numbers, a whole series of numbers evolves. For example, when zero combines with number 1, the numbers 11 through 19 that belong to that series evolve. * The introduction of zero aided the development of math, science and the modern technology that brought mankind to the computer age, but it does not "exist."*

In numerology each number is connected to the elements like: **Ether, Air, Water, Fire, and Earth.**

0=Ether/ * 4 & 5=Air * 2 & 7= Water * 6 & 8=Earth * 1, 3 & 9=Fire

Note: 0 (zero) is all and nothing at the same time.

Remember— NOTHING IS SOMETHING in Ancient Science!

I am still wondering who decided during **"Reconstruction"** to make the zero (0) not a number—when clearly without it we wouldn't be able to perform various mathematical equations. *(This is just my opinion)*

We have to continue to seek knowledge, wisdom, over-standing and balance. Or what is called Ma'at— (Truth, Justice, Righteousness, Balance and Reciprocity.) To find out more about the principles of Ma'at read, 'Nile Valley Contribution to Civilization,' ~ by Anthony T. Browder

MORE INFORMATION ABOUT ZERO

The following is a according to Wikipedia, the free encyclopedia:

Note: **Quoting Wikipedia does not mean it is a totally valid source— the reader must do their research and find a common thread of information that will guide you to the truth.**

*0 (zero; BrE: /'zɪərəʊ/ or AmE: /'ziːroʊ/) is both a **number**[1] and the **numerical digit** used to represent that number in **numerals**. It fulfills a central role in **mathematics** as the **additive identity** of the **integers**, **real numbers**, and many other algebraic structures. As a digit, 0 is used as a placeholder in **place value systems**. In the English language, 0 may be called **zero**, **nought** or (US) **naught** /'nɔːt/, **nil**, or — in contexts where at least one adjacent digit distinguishes it from the letter "O" — **oh** or o /'oʊ/. Informal or slang terms for zero include **zilch** and **zip**.[2] Ought or aught /'ɔːt/ has also been used historically.*

Etymology
*Main articles: **Names for the number 0** and **Names for the number 0 in English***

*The word zero came via French zéro from Venetian zero, which (together with cypher) came via Italian zefiro from Arabic صفر, ṣafira = "it was empty", ṣifr = "zero", **"nothing"**. The first known English use was in 1598.*

*In 976 AD the Persian encyclopedist **Muhammad ibn Ahmad al-Khwarizmi,** in his "Keys of the Sciences", remarked that if, in a calculation, no number appears in the place of tens, then a little circle should be used "to keep the rows". This circle was called صفر (ṣifr, "empty") in Arabic language. That was the earliest mention of the name ṣifr that eventually became **zero**.[8]*

The following is more interesting information about the Meaning of Number Zero ~ from www.spiritualmeaningofnumbers.com
Written by A. Venefica on November 5th, 2007

The symbolic meaning of number zero alludes to: Mystery, Nothingness, Infinity, Potential, Possibility, Eternity, Reflection, Void, Totality, and Rebirth.

*"Primarily, the spiritual meaning of zero deals with **pure potentiality**. It is the point from which all other numbers spring forth. Even visually – the number zero is symbolic of the seed, womb or egg from which pure potential emerges.*

Because the zero also visually resembles a circle, this is symbolic of eternity, evolution, infinity. Additionally, as with most symbols comprised or containing the circle we're dealing with meanings of cycles, evolution, and time. Think wheels here – "what comes around goes around."

However, due to its numerical value, the zero may also be interpreted as a void – a representation of non-existence, and sometimes death. But, again, our minds wander back to the symbolism of eternity and infinity as well as cycles and rebirth. Consequently we may say there is no real death only another phase of life.

*Mayan glyphs used the "cosmic spiral" to represent the numeral zero – they inherently knew the **massiveness of mystery** swirling in the pools of zero-ness.*

Pythagoras, (practically the father of numerology) viewed the sign of the zero as the container for all things and the birthing place of all other values (that which proceeds must be the birth giver of all that follows). This is also the interpretation of the zero in Tarot numbers as well as other mystery school teachings.

*Focus upon the zero is encouraged when we wish to be present in the moment, when we are trying to **regroup our level of awareness**. This is because the zero is representative of the essence of reality. It is everything and nothing at the same time.*

As you can see – just from this brief summary, the concepts of the spiritual meaning of zero are heady indeed. When we begin to contemplate zero we soon find ourselves on an endless adventure."

The previous info is for research purposes only!

Numbers R Simple…People are Complicated Tip D:

Numbers are not the ending of your studies but, the beginning—find a common thread that helps you learn what is needed to better yourself and others around you

∗∗∗∗∗∗∗∗∗∗∗∗

1 One

The Individual / Individuality

The *simplicity* of those born on the 1st, 10th, 19th or 28th of the month is considered a number **1** person connected to the Sun. People born connected to frequency **#1** are the leaders in the world. They are the ***individuals, the trail blazers, and the one who love to win and dislike losing in any way.*** They usually take the spot light and don't like to lose in any competition. When you are in a race we all strive to be **#1**. Although **#2** and **#3** are rewarded in some cases—nothing beats **#1** and its reward. Number **1** people usually work well on their own or they are always propelled to the top of their field or the class. Like all numbers there is a Ying & Yang, a positive & negative, a good & bad, etc. Whatever you may identify it with there is always a balance. Although the number one are leaders they are also very creative, focused, direct and straight forward—so much so that some may have a problem with them but that is just who they are.

The *complications* **of the number 1 person** can be arrogant, bossy, procrastinators, manipulative, controlling, challenging & insulting and can be a detriment to their own growth due to a lack a vision and encouragement from people around them.

Note: **All people connected to the same numbers are not exactly the same but each of them has a common thread that they follow especially when they are associated with a compound number. Which we will discuss in Chapter 6 called, 'Compound / Composite numbers.' In that chapter you will see how an added number changes one's frequency.**

2 Two

The Companion / Union

The *simplicity* of those born on the 2nd, 11th, 20th, or 29th of the month are considered a number **2** person connected to the Moon. The **#2** person is a duality number, a number of help, assistance, union and companionship. Number **2** are always willing to help without hesitation. Those born with that number are the natural companions in any relationship... whether in love or business they are one of the best numbers to work with. Usually misunderstood in their relationships due to their wanting to be of help to others around them.

The *complications* of the number 2 person can be indecisive, doubtful, and clingy or not a team player because of how they were treated and how it affected them while growing up. The **#2** person must learn to stay away from flattery and be conscious of the friends they keep. (Especially from the opposite sex) Protect your emotions because when you are emotionally involved you tend to waste needed energy.

Note: There are also those born with the compound numbers with the number 1, 2 or as a lead number or ending number. Like: 10, 19, 20, 21, 29, 30 or 31th of the month. (Of which I will discuss in Chapter 6 about Compound / Composite numbers)

3 Three

The Expression / Expressive

The *simplicity* of those born on the 3ʳᵈ, 12ᵗʰ, 21ˢᵗ, or 30ᵗʰ of the month are considered a number 3 person. The **#3** is a fire number commonly connected to Jupiter. Those connected to **3** are usually very expressive in many ways, very talkative and full of energy. They love expansion, growth and seek understanding in many fields. According to lessons of ***the Nation of Gods and Earths*** *(derive from the teachings of the Most Hon. Elijah Muhammad)* The **#3** is **Understand (or Understanding)** and those under that number seeks it in life through art, writing, speaking, etc. They have a very passionate and high strung way of connecting with the masses or just in small circles. They are excellent hosts and hostesses of functions of all kinds.

The *complications* **of the number 3 person** can be extreme worriers, whiners, criticizers, extravagant, vain, exaggerators and superficial. They highly express these negatives to the point of annoyance. They also should avoid being a tyrant, pessimistic, undependable, wasteful and boastful.

4 Four

The Foundation / Structure

The *simplicity* of those born on the 4ᵗʰ, 13ᵗʰ, 22ⁿᵈ, or 31ˢᵗ of the month is considered a number **4** person connected to Uranus. The number **4** person is supposed to be structured in what they do. Like the four corners of the square.... they are to lay the foundation of their life by planning what they do in order to be successful in life. The **4** are good for communications in the media and they are loyal, patient, trust worthy and enduring. Because the **#4** is an air number connected to the sign Aquarius it has an eccentric way of seeing or communicating outside of the scope of others.... which would be considered weird.

The *complications* **of the number 4 person** can be narrow minded, unstructured, dogmatic, misunderstood due to miscommunication. If they do not structure their life they can be destructive to themselves and others. They can become restricted in their own mind, which will create limitation. They must learn to be open minded, focused and organized.

5 Five

The Versatile / Change

The *simplicity* **of those born on the 5ᵗʰ, 14ᵗʰ, or 23ʳᵈ of the month** are considered a number **5** person connected to Mercury. The freedom loving number 5...their motto should be, *"Born free— free as the birds fly...Free as the wind blows."* They are all about change, movement and constant flow. If you ever get into a conversation with a 5 you will notice that they love to talk and know about many things. Sometimes they can be a "**jack-of-all-trades** and **master of none,**" if they are not focused. They are very brilliant with many talents. They are adaptable, clever, social butter flies, travelers and love variety. They should be encouraged to master one talent at a time or use the first masterful accomplishment (or gift) and carry the rest through the gate.

The *complications* **of the number 5 person** can be procrastinators, rushing, careless, inconsistent and abusive of their freedom. They should avoid straining themselves, letting stress over take them, over indulgence of various kinds of drugs, sex, alcohol, and other vices. They can be very irresponsible if not taught the value of responsibility from young.

6 Six

The Balance / Family

The *simplicity* **of those born on the 6ᵗʰ, 15ᵗʰ, or 24ᵗʰ of the month** is considered a number **6** person connected to Venus. The number **6** person are sensual, seeks balance, family, understanding, home, loving and are lovers of beautiful earthly things. Usually, youthful, very beautiful or handsome individuals and they have beautiful energy when cultivated properly. People love to get advice from the **6** person because they always give balance to every situation. They are very magnetic; service orientated and natural consultants. If you plan on working with or dating a number 6 person they are known for their taste in clothing, shoes and some consider them very high maintenance.

The *complications* of the number 6 person can be worriers, cynical, and egotistical. They must learn to avoid anxiety and should shun arguments. They should not rush and they should stay away from emotional drama. Learn to not hold grudges or it will affect you. Remember, forgiveness is the highest form of healing.

7 Seven

The Researcher / Meditative

The *simplicity* of those born on the 7th, 16th, or 25th of the month are considered a number **7** person connected to Neptune. The number **7** person are the great researchers, spiritualist, quiet storms and very intuitive. Number **7** people are usually very emotional but are known to be shy (but they are not); they are just observing their surroundings. Their silent wisdom speaks volumes in time—as long as they stay focused, spiritual and aware of their capabilities. If they learn to follow their gut feelings, watch and listen more before they speak—they will excel in various fields of life.

The *complications* of the number 7 person can be considered cold, aloof, worrywarts, humiliating, sarcastic, confusing and erratic. They can also be known as a faultfinder. In time, they must learn to use their psychic abilities for the good of man and to be a guiding light to the world.

8 Eight

The Power / Executive

The *simplicity* of those born on the 8th, 17th, or 26th of the month are considered a number 8 person connected to Saturn. The money attractor, the power giant, the executive extraordinaire is what the **8** person is and does in their *"Right Mind."* These people will always attract material wealth, money and power but have to learn to master money from all levels (spiritual & physical) from the ground up. The **#8** person always seem to have it (finance) but it always seems to slip through their fingers because of the lack of discipline. If the **8** person can stay organized, controlled and maintain a positive attitude to succeed—they will have no problem generating money through a structured and spiritual base.

The *complications* of the number 8 person can be a lover of power, careless and sometimes considered revengeful, cold and heartless. They should not let their love for money be their driving force. If they don't maintain control… material strain and intolerance will consume them. Avoid poor judgment and wasted energy. Injustice, bullying, and abuse of any kind will be your down fall.

9 Nine

The Completion / Universality

The *simplicity* of those born on the 9th, 18th, or 27nd of the month are considered a number 9 person connected to Mars. The completion on the number chart, the number of completeness and love. The 9 are in love with LOVE. But, don't get on their bad side because just as much as they can show their warmth as the last of the fire numbers on the chart—they can also show their anger that can be compared to a rapidly out of control burning building. The number 9 person is energetic, inspirational, daring, universal, and straight forward and to the point. When you want an honest answer to any question—go to the # 9 person in most cases because it is hard for them to beat-around-the-bush—so to speak.

The *complications* of the number 9 person can be aimless in goals, fickle, ego driven, quick tempered, impractical and impulsive and sometimes narrow minded. Learn to avoid pointless dreaming and see a goal to its completion. The 9 person must stay away from arguments, weapons, fire, over-indulgence and vulgarity. Always take the higher road.

11 Eleven

Spiritual Mastery / Illumination

The *simplicity* of those born on the 11th of the month are considered a Master number 11 person. This master number is of a spiritual awakening and these people should pay attention to their dreams because they are educated through them. The **11** are the ones who bring light to the world by connecting the spiritual to the physical. They are very brilliant, in tuned and highly intuitive to the point that some may consider them crazy or let's say, **"out-of-the-ordinary."** The **11** can revert to **#2 (1+1=2)** which reduces the strength of the master number but we will discuss this further in *Chapter 5 ~ Master Numbers.*

The *complications* **of the number 11 person** can be aimless, over-sensitive, careless, deceptive, pessimistic and dishonest. In order to operate on the master level of this number they must learn to see things to its finish. Also, they should avoid indecisiveness and laziness. *(Also view the complications of the number 2)*

22 Twenty-Two

Material Mastery / Master Builder

The *simplicity* **of those born on the 22nd of the month** are considered a Master number **22** person. The **22** are the master builders of the world. They are very intuitive and are known to lay a major foundation in various businesses—like: music, communication, etc. They are on the top of their fields in every endeavor and nothing can really hold them back but themselves. As they are maturing from childhood to adulthood they should be encouraged to be their very best and stay focused and structured. Now, the **22** can revert to **#4 (2+2=4)** which reduces the strength of the master number but we will discuss this further in *Chapter 5 ~ Master Numbers.*

The *complications* **of the number 22 person** can be harsh, insensitive, cruel, overly stern, moody, restless, impatient, hateful and boring. They must learn to avoid doubting themselves, being secretive, having an inferiority complex, criminal activities, and being vile and vicious. Steer clear of unsupportive people (family, friends, etc.) and get-rich-quick schemes are not your specialty—so stay away from it. *(Also view the complications of the number 4)* ☺

CHAPTER 5

"Mastering one's self through constant study—is the ultimate goal." ~ Dr. Phil Valentine

MASTER NUMBERS

(Their Strengths & Weaknesses)

According to a dear friend and numerologist, Lloyd Strayhorn author of **'Numbers and You'** he states, *"There are basically two master numbers, the 11 and the 22. These two numbers, under "modern" Numerology, possess certain powers and should never be reduced to the single numbers of 2 or 4. Persons born on the 11th or 22nd of the month possess the qualities of leadership and inspiration..."*

I agree with the above statement but the interesting thing about people connected with *masters' numbers* is that many of them don't realize their potential and unknowingly revert to the single digit of their master number. *(For example 11=1+1 = 2 and 22=2+2 = 4)*

Just like any number they (the master #) have their strengths and weaknesses. All numbers have their strengths and

45

weaknesses how-so-ever, people vibrating under master #s have been given an extra dose due to the doubling of the numbers like: *11, 22, 33, 44, 55,* and so on.

The repeating of the number gives it more energy and potential for success and failure depending on the person that possesses the master number and their drive, motivation, endurance, background, inner conversation and more. Yes, it is true, people born under any of the numbers can reach their highest potential and those vibrating under the master #s have been given an earthly opportunity to show their mastery on multiple levels. It is like giving a person extra powers and without proper guidance from the family or their surroundings it can be easily reduced to the single digit vibration of the master number which would lessen the strength and allow the weakest vibration of the number to come to being.

Numbers R Simple...People are Complicated Tip E:

People who carry the master numbers in their chart are very powerful and should be guided to the highest expression of that number to be successful.

For instance observe the chart below:

Master Number to Single digits

00 ----------------------0

11----------------------2

22----------------------4

33----------------------6

44----------------------8

55----------------------1

66----------------------3

77----------------------5

88----------------------7

99----------------------9

After looking at the above chart I shall quote Pastor A.R. Bernard, *"Strengthen your Strengths and manage your Weaknesses."*

There are also instances where people connected to master #s—whether through personality or their life path numbers, often revert to their lower number by default or because they do not want to live up to the responsibilities of the master #. Usually when I speak to someone born on a master number like **11** or **22**— I try to explain to them the importance of vibrating on the master energy of which they're born.

Below are a few Master number carriers:

The following information is from Wikipedia, I encourage the reader to analyze Mr. Cooke and the strange/weird circumstance surrounding his death and how his numbers play a part. Please notice the master numbers and think about the numbers you come up with and YOU will know that it is deeper than what is being said. It is all mathematical when I read it.

*"Sam Cooke born **January 22, 1931 and died at the age of 33 on December 11, 1964**, at the Hacienda Motel at **9137** South Figueroa Street in Los Angeles, California. Answering separate reports of a shooting and of a kidnapping at the motel, police found Cooke's body, clad only in a sports jacket and shoes but no shirt, pants or underwear. He had sustained a gunshot wound to the chest; with it later determined that the bullet had pierced his heart. The motel's manager reported that she had shot Cooke in self-defense after he broke into her office residence and attacked her. However, the details of the case involving Cooke's death have remained in dispute."*

Jan. 22, 1931 ~ 1+2+2+1+9+3+1=19 (1+9=1+0=1 is his Life Path)

1+2+2+1+9+6+4=25 (2+5=7 He was in his # 7 year Meditative)

The Day he died: 1+2+1+1+1+9+6+4=25 (2+5=7 He died on a 7 day)

Remember the age he passed on... 33 (another master number)

*Note: When I read into Sam Cooke through numbers I see where he should have stayed to himself and away from people. **Introspection, spiritual development through focus-thought and research was the order of the # 7. He was also in his critical cycle before his 34th (3+4=7) birthday.** Refer to 'Numbers and You' by Lloyd Strayhorn. Page 118 – 120.*

I also read that there was something very secretive & strange behind the whole scenario. In other words—there is a lot *more to the story. Remember, the number 4 attracts secret enemies and Mr. Cooke was born on January **22 (2+2=4).** Is this a coincidence? I think not!* **Things that make you say, HMMMM!**

Other Master number carriers like:

*Shaggy born October **22** (Master #), 1968*

> *1+0+2+2+1+9+6+8=29 2+9 = 11 **(Master #)** 1+1 = 2*

(single digit)

Please note the master numbers in Shaggy's birthday (Personality & Life Path)

Shaggy and I went to Erasmus Hall H.S. in the 80's and back then he showed great potential as an artist in Flatbush Brooklyn, NY. He had a way to communicate his lyric to his audience that was *odd, creative and fun*—which is not by coincidence. Usually, those born connected to the number **22** have the **#4** energy attached and the **#4** has a weird way of communicating—especially with the opposite sex.

Mr. Strayhorn stated in 'Numbers and You,' *"…It has the power to make or break, depending on the person holding this number. In Astrology, the master number **22** is governed by the Zodiac sign of Aquarius, the water bearer.*

*Those carrying the **22** in their names or birth dates must learn the right use of its power, for the **22** can tear down and destroy as well as build. Precision, accuracy, analysis, and determination are strongly associated with the number **22**. A **22** person usually has a strong mechanical turn of mind and* *the power to succeed in whatever areas of interest are the strongest.*

*The **22** is composed of two **2**s. The **2** by itself represents the Moon and is inventive, artistic, and imaginative. However, when you add up **2** + **2**, you get the single number **4**. This represents the planet Uranus, which governs odd and unusual things, social questions of all kinds, new schools of thought, and the like..."*

The number **4** is an air number and is also a ***feminine*** number. Thus, it is not surprising that Shaggy's music is geared towards ***women*** and he has been very successful promoting his music to women.

Note*: The diamond selling album which cleared the path for him to move from Reggae Artist to now Pop/Reggae Artist was an album that featured his very popular song, **"It Wasn't Me."***

Another reggae artist connected to the master number **22** is **Beenie Man** who was born on **August 22, 1973.**

8+2+2+1+9+7+3 = 32 and 3+2 = 5 (Life Path)

Beenie Man has a very extraordinary way of communicating with his audience—especially women. *Note that his life path #5 which represents change, promotion, and multi-talented.*

Again, **22 (2+2=4)** and the **#4** rules over the weird, unexpected and have an odd way of attracting people. Also, numbers **22** or **4** can find themselves in weird situations that make things complicated and create limitations. My advice to individuals born with master numbers is to seek information in regards to the master numbers to best guide them throughout life. Also, analyze those who share the same numbers—especially successful people. Their success didn't come in a vacuum. Most of them operated on an instinctive sense of surety that they realized from young. And, they are those who were heavily into charting and finding out more about who they are from a metaphysical level.

Another **master number** carrier is **Minister Louis Farrakhan, born:**

May 11, 1933 (5+1+1+1+9+3+3=23)

He is a master orator, which is revealed, through his #11 (a master number) that tell us many things about his ability to communicate on a higher level. Thus, he is the spiritual head and leader of The Nation of Islam. Also, his life path is a number **5** and for years he has been able to promote and adapt to change—which also explains why he does what he does. *Promotion* and **change** are two of the known qualities of the **number 5 person.**

Another person connected to the master #11 is Dancehall sensation **Elephant Man (O'Neil Bryan) born:**

September 11, 1975 (9+1+1+1+9+7+5 = 33) *Note: 3+3 = 6*

Elephant Man's success with dance tunes has created a whole craze amongst the youth in our communities and around the world was not a surprise to me when I found out his birthday and read his numbers. Number **11** people bring light or illumination to something that was suppressed or concealed.

When Dancehall was going through its *killing & gun phase*—Elephant man brought the dancing back into the clubs. He was able to bring the dancing culture again with more vigor, excitement and allowed the fun to come back into Dancehall music, which was sparked by late dancehall artist/dancer **Mr. Bogle**.

Note: Mr. Bogle (Gerald Levy) was born on August 22, 1964—also connected to a master number. 8+2+2+1+9+6+4 = 32 (3+2=5) * I can't make this up.

****

The following chart is for those who would like to find out their **universal year**. To find it—just add your month and day to the number of the year below and keep adding until you get to a **single digit**.

UNIVERSAL POWER CHART FOR EACH YEAR

2000 = 2	2011 = 4	2022 = 6
2001 = 3	2012 = 5	2023 = 7
2002 = 4	2013 = 6	2024 = 8
2003 = 5	2014 = 7	2025 = 9
2004 = 6	2015 = 8	2026 = 1
2005 = 7	2016 = 9	2027 = 11
2006 = 8	2017 = 1	2028 = 3
2007 = 9	2018 = 11	2029 = 4

2008 = 1	**2019 = 3**	**2030 = 5**
2009 = 11	**2020 = 4**	**2031 = 6**
2010 = 3	**2021 = 5**	**2032 = 7**

Note: Refer to the explanation of numbers in this book or the other recommended books in the back. ☺

CHAPTER 6

"Seek balance and harmony in all that you do." ~ King Simon

COMPOUND / COMPOSITE NUMBERS (10 – 31)

The importance of compound (or composite) numbers is spoken about by a few numerologists because certain practitioners would rather recognize the single digit energy of the compound number than acknowledge the vibration of each number's influence within the compound number itself.

Many wonder if the numbers after **9** (such as **10, 11, 12, 13, 22,** etc.) have any significant difference than their single digit counter-part. Well, this is where I quote the title of this book, *"Numbers R Simple... People are Complicated,"* in regards to how each number in the compound can affect the persons connected to them. Over the years I have recognized that people born on dates from **10 to 31** are somewhat different than those connected to the **single dates only**. In this chapter we will briefly cover the added characters discovered in the person who possess the compound (or composite) numbers not usually found in those connected to numbers **1 to 9**. Although planets are a factor and connected to each number—*our focus will simply stay within the elements. **Such as:** Ether, Fire, Earth, Air and Water. **Note:** ether is void or womb and connected to the zero.*

0 > 1 > 2 > 3 > 4 > 5 > 6 > 7 > 8 > 9

(FROM BEGINNING TO ENDING 0 - 9)

****

Numbers R Simple…People are Complicated Tip F:

Always identify each number within all compound numbers because, the vibration connected to each number is very significant and must be analyzed for further understanding of the individuals.

****

Below is a brief meaning of Compound Numbers and how their elements affect the people connected to them:

10 = *Fire* + *Ether* = *Extreme Fire Energy:* Success, constructive, dominating, leadership, pioneer and extreme in both ways.

~ **On the *complicated* side of those born on the 10th** can be overly arrogant, destructive and leaders of corruption in more ways than one.

11 = *Fire + Fire = Air or Water (Depending on its 11 or 2 use):* Creativity, Inspiring, spiritual and highly intuitive master.

~ **On the *complicated* side of those born on the 11th** can be the master of deception and a master thief. If they allow the **2** energy in **(1+1=2)** they can be bad tempered with a tendency to lie for no reason.

12 = *Fire + Water = Fire:* Leader, creative, natural partner, youthful companion and expansive.

~ **On the *complicated* side of those born on the 12th** can be a walking contradiction due to the fire and water element in their compound number. They can be a deceptive bully, a tyrant and a mischief maker.

13 = *Fire + Fire = Air:* Leader, expression and a need for structure and organization.

~ **On the *complicated* side of those born on the 13th** can be a fire ball of fearfulness, a worrier, violent and hateful.

14 = *Fire + Air = Air:* Leader, structure, foundation and adaptable to change.

~ **On the *complicated* side of those born on the 14th** can be ego driven, impractical, irresponsible and over indulging in substance abuse and sex.

15 = *Fire + Air = Earth:* Creative leader—who improvises well and is able to intuitively bring about family harmony and balance.

~ **On the *complicated* side of those born on the 15ᵗʰ** can be lazy, careless, jealous and suspicious of every little thing.

16 = *Fire + Earth = Water:* Leader of the home with an intuitive & spiritual base.

~ **On the *complicated* side of those born on the 16ᵗʰ** can be arrogant, self-righteous, deceitful and very suppressive of their thoughts which can cause depression.

17 = *Fire + Water = Earth:* Pioneering qualities with spiritual insight that will help to achieve material gain.

~ **On the *complicated* side of those born on the 17ᵗʰ** can be stubborn, loud, abusive, contradictory, moody, cold and very power hungry & careless.

18 = *Fire + Earth = Fire:* Head strong leader and executive with a loving, selfless nature that needs to see things to completion.

~ **On the *complicated* side of those born on the 18ᵗʰ** can be antagonistic, stubborn, strenuous, inconsistent and very emotionally unbalanced.

19 = *Fire + Fire = Fire:* Creative leadership that will see things to completion and must use love to be successful.

~ **On the *complicated* side of those born on the 19ᵗʰ** can be overly selfish, manipulative, vulgar & bitter and can develop instabilities.

Reminder: The number 1 adds an extra "Self Ego" dynamic to the number it proceeds in the above compound numbers.

20 = *Water + Ether = Intense Water Energy:* Natural companion and very service orientated, cooperative and loving. But this can go both ways if not balanced.

~ **On the *complicated* side of those born on the 20ᵗʰ** can be overly deceptive, petty, cruel and very insincere.

21 = *Water + Fire = Fire:* Intuitive partner with a creative and expressive flow of energy for anything involving the arts. *(Like Writing, speaking, acting, etc.)*

~ **On the *complicated* side of those born on the 21ˢᵗ** can be careless, petty, sometimes vain and hypocritical.

22 = *Water + Water = Air:* Highly intuitive with a strong mastery of the material world.

~ **On the *complicated* side of those born on the 22ⁿᵈ** can be indifferent, a criminal, insensitive, vulgar and a master of destruction.

23 = *Water + Fire = Air:* Spiritual partnership, awareness of expression and a need to maintain their youthful freedom.

~ **On the *complicated* side of those born on the 23ʳᵈ** can be a procrastinator, deceptive, slack, and abusive and also over indulgent of sex and drugs.

24 = *Water + Air = Earth:* Intuitive, loving, structured and a need for balance and harmony.

~ **On the** *complicated* **side of those born on the 24th** can be a hoarder, pessimist, self-righteous and suspicious.

25 = *Water* + *Air* = *Water:* Strong intuition with a free will to learn the spiritual mysteries of life.

~ **On the** *complicated* **side of those born on the 25th** can be too secretive, disgruntled, cunning, confusing, contradictory and erratic.

26 = *Water* + *Earth* = *Earth:* Partnership and harmony with earthly intuition with remarkable executive abilities to accomplish great things.

~ **On the** *complicated* **side of those born on the 26th** can be strenuous, impatient, abusive and unscrupulous.

27 = *Water* + *Water* = *Fire:* Intuitively devoted partner with a direct energetic way of accomplishing goals and success.

~ **On the** *complicated* **side of those born on the 27th** can be bitter, cruel, overly emotional, very argumentative, deceptive and very moody.

28 = *Water* + *Earth* = *Fire:* Partnership and material gain will make them the leader in whatever their mind sets out to achieve.

~ **On the** *complicated* **side of those born on the 28th** can be over exaggerating, selfish, a living & breathing contradiction, very manipulating and revengeful.

29 = *Water + Fire = Air (or Water 2+9=11 & 1+1=2)*: Spiritual awareness with energy, love and drive will allow you to be a master of your destiny.

~ On the *complicated* side of those born on the 29th can be dishonest, degrading, shiftless, deceptive and vulgar.

Reminder: The number 2 adds an extra "Partnering Ego" dynamic to the number it proceeds in the above compound numbers.

30 = *Fire + Ether = Excessive Fire Energy*: An overly expressive nature (in work or play) success can be achieved over time and must be worthy and Positive.

~ On the *complicated* side of those born on the 30th can be overly jealous, critical of self & others, wasteful, hypocritical and filled with silly pride.

31 = *Fire + Fire = Air*: Emotionally expressive in a weird way and have leadership abilities with a need to be stable and organized.

~ On the *complicated* side of those born on the 31st can be destructive, narrow-minded, intolerant, emotionally limited and repressive.

Reminder: The number 3 adds an extra "Expressive Ego" dynamic to the number it proceeds in the above compound numbers.

Note: The previous meaning of Compound Numbers is just a brief outlook that you can research. Planets and their connection to numbers are also important. Take your time to study the symbolism of Compound Numbers known as 'The Tarot System.' I will provide resources and recommended reading in the back of this book. ☺

CHAPTER 7

"One thing about Universal Principles—they never go out of style." ~ Lloyd Strayhorn

NUMBERS CONNECTION TO HEALTH, NAMES & WORDS

It has always amazed me how numbers are connected to words, and how they actually bring out the intent of the *word, name, place, thing and even health.* Numbers are exciting to me all the time. Lloyd Strayhorn always says, *"If you can count on your fingers and toes—then you can do numerology."* My greatest feeling about **numerology** and various ancient **"occult"** sciences is what it does for one's *self-awareness, self-knowledge, guidance and mathematical* connection to life— to me it is un-matched in this area of one's development.

Numbers R Simple

In this chapter we will touch on **NUMBERS** and its simple connection to our **HEALTH, NAMES & WORDS** we use.

Health is a very important part of each of our lives and we cannot do anything without good health. When I teach on the trains and buses of New York, I find that my health presentations are well responded to. I think everyone, in their right mind, knows that maintaining good health is necessary for various accomplishments in life. Really, think about it. *If you were sick and unable to move would you be able to enjoy the things you love to do?* Like, vacations, dinner at your favorite restaurant, and movie night with a friend or family member or even walking through a park. The answer is NO! Be under no illusions your health is the most important part of living in this realm.

Well, did you know that certain natural herbs, fruits, vegetables and plants are connected to planets and months of the year, which correspond to the numbers of our birth?

This science is ancient and has been used by our ancestors for over tens of thousands of years. *Have you ever wonder why certain fruits, vegetables and herbs grow in different seasons?* There is a reason but I am going to keep it simple in this chapter. **I will have other resources in the back of this book for your continual research.**

"Remember, these ancient sciences do not take you away from your belief or knowledge of the Creator— it can only make you a better religious person in the Creator's sight if used for positive means." ~ *King Simon*

The previous statement is for those who are seeking answers and are still connected to main stream religions like: **Christianity, Islam or Judaism.**

Below we will use the Chaldean and Pythagorean numerical charts:

Chaldean System							
1	**2**	**3**	**4**	**5**	**6**	**7**	**8**
A	B	C	D	E	U	O	F
I	K	G	M	H	V	Z	P
J	R	L	T	N	W		
Q		S		X			
Y							

Pythagorean System								
1	**2**	**3**	**4**	**5**	**6**	**7**	**8**	**9**
A	B	C	D	E	F	G	H	I
J	K	L	M	N	O	P	Q	R
S	T	U	V	W	X	Y	Z	

****

Numbers R Simple

Below are numbers and their connection to your health:

The 1 person ~ can have Heart issues like: Irregular circulation, palpitation and high blood pressure. They can also suffer from eye problems or astigmatism. *You should check your eyesight regularly.* **The Herbs, Fruits & Vegetables are:** *Chamomile, bay leaves, cloves, nut-meg, sorrel, lavender, ginger, thyme, dates, oranges, lemons, barley, apples, figs, kale and honey. Avoid foods that will clog your system.* **Look out for possible health issues in January, May, October and December.**

The 2 person ~ can suffer from all types of stomach and digestive issues. They must be careful of ptomaine poisoning, gastric issues, bowel problems and internal growths of all kinds. *Get regular check-ups and drink plenty of water.* **The Herbs, Fruits & Vegetables are:** *Cabbages, apples, carrots, lettuce, turnips, cucumber, melon, kale, strawberries, lemons, linseed, turnips and okra. Leave the extra spicy foods out of your diet.* **Look out for possible health issues in January, February, April, July and November.**

The 3 person ~ can suffer from nervous issues and overstrain of the nervous system. Be careful of developing various forms of skin problems, low blood pressure, foot issues and kidney problems. *Do not over-work yourself.* **The Herbs, Fruits & Vegetables are:** *Beets, berries, asparagus, dandelions, sage, lungwort, cherries, figs, almonds, mint and comfrey.* **Look out for possible health issues in February, June, August, September and December.**

The 4 person ~ can suffer from mysterious ailments that are difficult to diagnose. You can have mental issues and head, back; bladder and kidneys pains are possible. Be mindful of depression. Try to stay away from highly seasoned meals and red meat. *Hypnosis is a recommended treatment.* **The Herbs, Fruits & Vegetables are:** *Spinach, sage, coconut, lentils, bananas, marigold, romaine, pilewort and Solomon's seal.* **Look out for possible health issues in January, February, May, July, August, September and October.**

The 5 Person ~ can suffer from nervous problems, mental fatigue, insomnia, twitching in parts of the face, eyes, hands and possible paralysis. *Get plenty of rest and solitude. That is the best remedy.* **The Herbs, Fruits & Vegetables are:** *Sweet marjoram, parsley, carrots, thyme, walnuts, hazel-nuts, kale, rye, apricots, cherries and berries.*

Look out for possible health issues in June, September and December.

The 6 person ~ can suffer from throat, nose and sinus issues. The upper part of the lungs can be a problem, hay fever, blood circulation, bronchitis and asthma. Women connected to the number 6 should be mindful of any problems relating to your breast. *Get frequent checks ups and avoid fattening foods.* **The Herbs, Fruits & Vegetables are:** *Beans, parsnips, spinach, mint, melon, apples, peaches, motherwort, pomegranates, figs, almonds, thyme, rose-leaves, violets, dates and raspberries.* **Look out for possible health issues in January, February, April, May, August, October and November.**

The **7 person** ~ can suffer from too much worrying and being annoyed. They can also go through mental frustration and imagining the worst. Skin and minor stomach problems can be an issue. Pimples, boils and rashes can also develop if you eat anything that disagrees with your digestive system. *Relax, avoid moodiness and do not worry yourself sick.* **The Herbs, Fruits & Vegetables are:** *Lettuce, cabbage, mushrooms, cucumber, linseed, sorrel, apples, pineapples, honey, grapes, chicory, prunes, dates and onions.* **Look out for possible health issues in January, April, July and August.**

The **8 person** ~ can suffer from headaches, blood disorders, rheumatism, liver, bile, intestines and excretory issues. Concerns with the knees, teeth and bone can be problematic also. *They should stay clear of animal meat as much as possible and be careful of wrong medications and prescriptions. Keep away from lonely thoughts.* **The Herbs, Fruits & Vegetables are:** *Plantain, sage, ragwort, shepherd's purse, elder flower & berry, celery, spinach, figs, marshmallow, and carrots.* **Look out for possible health issues in January, February, June, July, August, September and December.**

The **9 Person** ~ can suffer from fevers, measles and chicken pox. You can be accident prone (Burns, cuts, bruises, car accidents, etc.). They should avoid spicy rich food and alcoholic beverages of all kind and steer clear of fires, guns, knives and explosives. *Stay away from over-indulgence of any vices. (Especially Alcohol)* **The Herbs, Fruits & Vegetables are:** Ginger, garlic, onions, pepper, wormwood, horse-radish, mustard-seed & greens, tomatoes, apples, rhubarb and eggplant. **Look out for possible health issues in January, April, May, July, October and November.**

****

Numbers R Simple…People are Complicated Tip G:

Research as much as you can in regards to your health and what is needed to maintain it. Always consult a Licensed Physician, Nutritionist or Certified Holistic Practitioner for necessary health advice.

****

The words we use daily have a vibration connected to them and depending on how we use them can determine if our communicational skill will be effective. The proceeding information is just a brief analysis of how words have numerical meanings and value. Each letter is connected to a number and each number is connected to a vibration that describes the number.

Below are a few words and their connection to numbers. We will use the Pythagorean System:

SALAAM ~ 1+1+3+1+1+4 = 11 = 2 (Harmony/Service/Love)

PEACE ~ 7+5+1+3+5 =21 = 3 (Expression/Kindness)

LOVE ~ 3+6+4+5 =18 = 9 (Selflessness/Magnetism/Love)

JUSTICE ~ 1+3+1+2+9+3+5 = 24 = 6 (Balance/Harmony/Healing)

HAPPINESS ~ 8+1+7+7+9+5+5+1+1 = 44= 8
(Structure/Money/Power)

HATE ~ 8+1+2+5 = 16 = 7 (Spiritual/Suppression)

DISASTER ~ 4+9+1+1+1+2+5+9 = 32 = 5

(Change/Life Experiences/Progressive)

HEAL ~ 8+5+1+3 = 17 = 8 (Success/Power/Control)

****

Our names are connected to numbers and some names are reflective of *power, money and executive energies* while another name might reflect *peace, harmony and love.* That is why when choosing **nicknames** you have to be careful— because, it can alter the vibration of the **birth name** either towards a positive or a negative. Some numerologist may use the **Chaldean System (C.S.)** and some may use the **Pythagorean System (P.S.).** I do not see any problems with using both. However, The *Chaldean System* has been a little more accurate when reading names and words.

I personally choose to use the one that resonates with my **personality** and **life path numbers in my birthday.** So, please use whichever **CHART** may work for you. **(Located at the beginning of this chapter)**

Below are a few names and their connection to numbers:

For example lets use my name using both systems:

SIMON ~ 3+1+4+7+5 = 20 = 2 **Water (C.S.)**

SIMON ~ 1+9+4+6+5 = 25 = 7 Water (P.S.)

My name under both systems is similar because 2 and 7 are water numbers.

YASIRA ~ 1+1+3+1+2+1 = 9 Fire (C.S.)

YASIRA ~ 7+1+1+9+9+1 = 28 = 10 = 1 Fire (P.S.)

The above name (Yasira) is under both systems and is similar because 9 and 1 are fire numbers. If I were to advise this person I would tell them that they should vibrate with the 9 energy because it has more universal appeal.

JORDAN ~ 1+7+2+4+1+5 = 20 = 2 Water (C.S.)

JORDAN ~ 1+6+9+4+1+5 = 17 = 8 Earth (P.S.)

The above name (Jordan) has a water and earth connection. I would advise them to vibrate with the 8 energy for success in business.

NICOLE ~ 5+1+3+7+3+5 = 24 = 6 Earth (C.S.)

NICOLE ~ 5+9+3+6+3+5 = 31 = 4 Air (P.S.)

The above name (Nicole) has an earth and air connection. Depending on their personality and life path—I would advise them to vibrate with the 6 energy for love, harmony and balance or the 4 energy if they wanted to maintain structure, organization, and communication. *The Number Charts Below will assist you.*

Chaldean System							
1	**2**	**3**	**4**	**5**	**6**	**7**	**8**
A	B	C	D	E	U	O	F
I	K	G	M	H	V	Z	P
J	R	L	T	N	W		
Q		S		X			
Y							

Pythagorean System								
1	**2**	**3**	**4**	**5**	**6**	**7**	**8**	**9**
A	B	C	D	E	F	G	H	I
J	K	L	M	N	O	P	Q	R
S	T	U	V	W	X	Y	Z	

Note: Consonants and vowels are also an important part of learning about your name. Resources are provided in the back of this book for further research. ☺

CHAPTER 8

"I have come to realize that the elements can work together on a higher level but, each element has a specific role."

~ King Simon Kweku

Numbers R Simple Relationship Chronicles

Numbers have an attractive vibration like signs in the zodiac and they also have a repelling vibration. Many years of observing signs in the zodiac and numbers have revealed that some are more harmonious with each other than others. Like fire signs such as Leo, Aries and Sagittarius are considered compatible because they're ruled by the same natural element. Also, there are those signs and numbers that are unharmonious with others— only due to the nature of elements in this physical realm.

It can be true that opposites attract in signs and numbers but an unharmonious relationship can be the result of such attraction in life if individuals don't understand their roles.

For example if you were born on the **17th** of the month—you are a number **8** person **(1+7=8 Earth number)** and the other person is born on the 4th of the month. This person would be considered a number **4** person (Air number).

Now, Earth **(8)** and Air **(4)** would not be considered a good combination due to the nature of the elements howsoever, if they understood their role and how they could work—it has great possibilities in business, communication and a structured foundation...just to name a few of the positives. If couples or partners lack the above over standing then problems will arise.

Also, the knowledge of the zodiac is important to determine how to make good connections in relationship, business, etc.

****
Numbers R Simple...People are Complicated Tip H:

Compound numbers (like 12, 23 or 31) and zodiac signs, can have distinctive results to an individual. So, please keep this in mind when attempting to learn more about people.

****

The Chronicles of a Number 1 person:

If you are born on the 1st, 10th, 19th, or 28th of the month, you are a number 1 person. This includes those under the sign of Leo.

The One and One Connective Energy:

These are the control freaks (so to speak) and when together the will of these two are strong and they are not afraid to stand strong together in companionship or business. Both are straight forward, direct and to the point with one another; even in the comfort of your own place, (bedroom, living room, bathroom, etc) you are not afraid to let each other know what you want or need. Now, those born on the **10th, 19th and 28th** might have a little extra due to the combination of numbers but, 1 is the over-all number they are connected to. Avoid selfishness and this can be a wonderful union. Months like February, April and August can be favorable— also days that add up to 1 are favorable and possibly **2** for a more achievable outcome.

The One and Two Connective Energy:

This combination is a one, two punch on one level—because the number **1** person is usually the leader in this relationship. The number **2** person is the natural companion and is very sensitive to the one person needs in every way. The number **1** (Sun) person shines its light for all to see and the number **2** (Moon) person reflects that light in more ways than one. The **1** person has to be sensitive to their partner's **(2 person)** needs if they want to keep them. The months that seem to work with both of you are February, July, and August—also days that add up to **1, 2 or 3** for attraction and unity.

The One and Three Connective Energy:

This couple's motto is, *"Work, Work, Work,"* because both are fire numbers with a lot of energy. There is a certain working understanding between these two and that is why their house-hole is usually empty because of their busy schedules. Both of you can be the life of the party but, number **1**'s will watch number **3**'s back while they flirtatiously work the room. If they understand each other's body language when in the public—it is smooth sailing straight to the bedroom. Your number **3** person finds it easy to shower you with titles of endearment if they feel you deserve it. A potentially good couple if they can stay focus and agreeable. Their best months are March, April, August and December—also days that add up to **1, 3 or 4** for more Structure.

The One and Four Connective Energy:

What an interesting blend of fire **(1)** and air **(4)** in this combination. Both of you have a magnetic draw to each other and in many ways you fuel each other like *Air fanning Flames*. The number **4** person and its special way of communicating grab the attention of the number **1** person because they admire their airy moods and unpredictable ways. The number **1**'s strength and focus helps the **4** person to structure and maintain solid ground. Try to avoid miscommunication and being insensitive to each other's need. During the intimate times both will have an energetic attitude in and out of the bedroom. So, have fun! The months you both share are February, April, and August—also days that add up to **1, 4 or 5** for change for the best.

The One and Five Connective Energy:

Yippy-Ki-Yah!!! When these two get together in their own weird way— they are very independent and both need their own space so they can adapt and improvise. They might even need their own room if they decided to live together. Now, number **1**, when dating a number **5** person—please don't get too much in their business by asking a whole host of questions…if you ever heard that song called, *'FLY LIKE AN EAGLE,'* well that is what a number **5** person will do if you place them in a Q & A session regarding their where-a-bouts. Your vibrations are beyond this world and both of you are not afraid to express yourselves in more ways than one and in more places than one. Your months to work it out are February, April, June, August and October also days that add up to **1, 5, or 6** for more harmony.

The One and Six Connective Energy:

This combination is a tricky one. Issues may arise because of controlling personalities— the **1** person being fire and the **6** person being earth. These numbers are in opposition to each other. It can work if both of you understood your roles from the beginning—because you both have your own personal manner that is yours. However, if both of you contemplate a long term relationship, that is a journey on its own. Number **1**'s love to give orders and it is usually in the mind set of, *"it's my way or the high way."* Number **6**'s are more the rulers of the home, family and see things from a more personal outlook. But, number **1**'s are not the kind to hold hands for a certain period of time. You are a leader, you are action orientated—whether in the business world or in the world of the bedroom. No shorts and straight to the point. In truth both of you don't share any months but you could probably connect on days like the **1ˢᵗ, 6ᵗʰ and 7ᵗʰ** of any month.

Note: Remember, this is in regards to numbers. If a zodiac was connected this can be a very different outcome.

The One and Seven Connective Energy:

This union would have to be based on leadership, spirituality or of the occult (which means Mystery) for it to work. Number **1**'s leadership qualities would have to mesh with number **7**'s depth of inner thoughts and introspection. Both would enjoy a house with their own individual rooms to call their own and create a room of love on various levels. This can be a very intimate and productive relationship if both are willing to understand each other's roles in their lives. Number **7** would maintain the spiritual base of the relationship while the number 1 maintains the business and up keep of the goals they have set together. In other words, "The Creator has to be the Center of this union." The two months that comes to mind in regards to the development and success of these numbers are February and July—also days that add up to **1, 7 or 8** for more success.

The One and Eight Connective Energy:

Business, business and more business is the strong point for these two numbers. **(1 & 8)** The emotional part of this combination will be leveled and respectful as long as they can maintain their business ventures. These two are usually in opposition to each other on one level but, on an enterprising level it could work. Their motto should be, *"Family is Business and Love is Law."* These two in numerology are giants on the mental plane for legacy, business and enterprise building. Many say both of you are like **"Mr. & Mrs. Freeze,"** but, that is furthest from the truth. In this union, *"the home is your throne"* to release the pressures of the day-to-day hustle and bustle—but, once talk is over the **'Sexual Healing'** song is on and popping with all the candle lights burning. There may not be any months to share but try to work it out on days of the month that lands on **1, 8, and 18**. This should add a little extra energy.

The One and Nine Connective Energy:

These two **(1 & 9)** are usually know as reflections of each other. They are the extremes on the number scale—making them one and the same. The Alpha **(*Opening*)** and the Omega **(*Conclusion*)**—in other words, if the number **1** person starts it—then the number 9 person will finish it. Both are fire and both are leaders in their own right. This will be a powerful couple as long as both can practice a healthy respect and a little give and take in this relationship. This is an ultimate combination when in an intimate setting. Fire! Is the element and straight forward love for each other is the guiding light. Heated months shared between these two are April, August and December—also days that add up to **1 and 9** are favorable.

The Chronicles of a Number 2 person:

If you are born on the 2nd, 11th, 20th or 29th, of any month, you are a number 2 person. This also includes those under the sign of Cancer.

The Two and One Connective Energy:

This is an interesting match because you can be indecisive and very sensitive, it is important that your partner offers you security and direction. If we delve into the elements of the numbers Water **(2)** and Fire **(1)** are somewhat attracted to each other but need a common ground for it to work in unison. And that common ground is appreciating the Moon and Sun attractive energy between the two numbers. **(2 & 1)** Remember, you're a natural companion and your number **1** partner is an adventurer and needs space every now-and-then to make it happen for the both of you. A good match if both can compromise and are able to stay in tune with each other's needs and goals. Months such as February, July and August are good for you to build. Also, days that add up to **2, 1, and 3** can be helpful**.**

The Two and Two Connective Energy:

There is an old saying, *"Water seeks its own level,"* and this is exactly what this combination is all about. You both would make a great couple with a very highly psychic connection. Even to the point that you would dream and think about similar things. There can be many ups and downs depending on each other's background, astrological sign and family history. But both of you can be the best of friends when you understand the importance of knowing each other's habit, strengths and weaknesses. This is especially so in the bedroom—let's say, *"Double the fun if neither of you run."* Your best months for your energies to connect are March, May, and July. Also, days that add up to the number **2 or 4** will help.

The Two and Three Connective Energy:

If you accept this social bunny and all of its expressive nature—it will more than likely benefit you in more ways than one. Number **3's** love to work as well as play. Your companionship and nurturing nature might have a problem with this to a certain degree. Now, if you can work with them **(3)** as they continue to expand their work load and if they can understand your **(2)** need for the closeness and protection— then this could be a working team or it could be a disaster. Both are emotional in their own way. Number **2** people are water and **3's** are fire and can boil and produce steam for the good or the bad of the relationship. May and October are the months that work for the both of you. Also, numbers that add up to **2, 3, and 5** can be a beneficial achievement.

The Two and Four Connective Energy:

What a bubbly combination these two make. Water exists in air just like air exists in water— for example H2O. Numbers **2 (water)** and **4 (air)** are multiplies of each other and as long as sensitive and companionship number **2** can deal with the structured and weird number **4**—it can work. Both of you are finicky about various things and sometimes number 4 can be moody; **MOODY + EMOTIONAL= A ROUGH JOURNEY.** Communication is really not a problem here as long as harmony is maintained. The months that you would be great together are February, July and August. Days that add up to **2, 4 and 6** would be an extra boost.

The Two and Five Connective Energy:

I don't think emotional number **2** can blend in well with the freedom loving number **5**. Depending on the zodiac—there is not enough adaptability in the world for these two. This relationship is easy to get in to but, hard when they get to know each other. Your number **2** nature is not going to go for number **5's** no-questions-asked attitude. If you even think the thought of number **5** rushing into marriage— you can forget about it! Sexually you are compatible but, how long do you think that will last if there is no solid commitment. The months you have in common are May, June, July and September. Also, think about days that add up to **2, 5, and 7** for a united combo.

The Two and Six Connective Energy:

These elements are considered harmony in motion. Water **(2)** and Earth **(6)** are a natural mix, that when blended positively—great things can manifest like: flowers, trees, etc. If there is no love & harmony then the relationship will become Mud. The sign of these individuals are also important. However, both are warm, considerate, love the family unit and very caring and sympathetic to each other's needs. **This might be too good to be true?** But, it all depends on both of you. If you stay in tune with each other and understand each other's backgrounds it will allow you both to maintain control, sensitivity and respect for a fulfilling relationship. Look towards March, May, July and October. Days that add up to **2, 6, and** maybe **8** will be of benefit.

The Two and Seven Connective Energy:

These water numbers are highly intuitive and very emotional in their own way. They can be very close if the **2** person can understand the number **7** person's need to be to themselves. This is a slow developing relationship because both of them have to get to know each other and be patient with one another. **Once these two open up to each other and establish a spiritual companionship—there is nothing**

that can't be accomplished. Your psychic energy is easily strengthened around water. Take a walk through the park or near a lake. This will bring a balance between the both of you. Water is the natural conduit between the spirit world and the physical world— Try to use it to your advantage— sexually and during meditation. Attempt to use March, May, July and October for leveling your water energies together— also days that add up to **2, 7** and maybe **9** for a more complete & loving experience.

The Two and Eight Connective Energy:

The magnetism of these two numbers is outstanding and can produce longevity on every level. Water **(2)** and Earth **(8)** makes a unifying combination to say the least. The number **2** person's companionship and sensitivity can blend well with the number **8** person's strong, executive diligence securely. This unit is a force to be reckoned with in every way. This is a sure *"Power Couple"* in business and a family legacy builder for their future. Sexual intimacy between you two is slow and growing but when it ignites—gets ready! The months to work it out are January, March, May, July and September. Days that add up to **2, 8** and **1** might be a workable achievement.

The Two and Nine Connective Energy:

Many say, *"Opposites Attract,"* but in this case—business, maybe… but, as far as relationship—possible but, wouldn't bet on it! This is the extreme water and fire elements. In business the number **2** person would be helpful to the number **9** but number **2** would have to look out for number **9's** temper or abusive attitude. Now, **depending on the**

astrological signs of the two—it could work but as far as these two numbers being intimate, **THIS CAN BE ALL DOWN HILL**. The **9** person is known for their universal love but they might not go for your emotional stress. Unless, there is clear understanding and if it is a business relationship with wealth involved. **(Still have to be cautious)** There are no months in common but, days to try it out on would be on the **2ⁿᵈ, 9ᵗʰ or 11ᵗʰ** of the month—just as a test.

The Chronicles of a Number 3 person

If you are born on the 3rd, 12th, 21st or 30th, of any month, you are a number 3 person. This also includes those under the signs of Sagittarius or Pisces.

The Three and One Connective Energy:

This double flamed combination is a tricky one. Both of you like to lead in more ways than one can imagine. The number **3** person is flirtatious and the number **1** person seeks the limelight. Your numbers are creative, popular, ambitious and dynamic but on the flip side you both can be vain, self-indulgent, arrogant and manipulative. If your number **3** expressive nature can come to grips with number **1's** sometimes cold and stand-offish nature—this could make a great team in all aspects. The months that will enhance your connection are February, April, August and December. Both of you are more than likely to enjoy days that add up to **3, 1** and maybe **4** for greater achievement.

The Three and Two Connective Energy:

An interesting situation can happen between these two numbers. *1. Either you will have a loving servant. 2. A companion that will support and give loving insight or 3. The*

#2 is a sensitive, unstable and indecisive water number that will dowse out your (#3) growing fire of expansion. The number **3** person is popular in many circles and both of them (**3 & 2**) together attract friends and like-minded company without difficulty. Emotions runs deep with these two number also—the **3** person has a fiery emotional energy and the number **2** person has a watery emotional energy which can collide if both individuals do not take time to really know each other in regards to family, friends and sensitive instabilities. Your love life should reign supreme once you understand the emotional needs of each other—and usually the **2** person loves taking orders in the bed. March, May, July, October and December are great for both of you. Days that add up to **3, 2** and **5** are good for an achieving moment of change.

The Three and Three Connective Energy:

This is a blazing fire waiting to happen. These two will probably never be home because they love to work and socialize. They are a *"Partying Animal House,"* so to speak—and function well at outings, social gatherings and networking events. Although both of you are reflections of each other your expressive emotions can get in the way if there is no understanding and tolerance. Intimate times will be passionate and well spent and enjoyable. Your best months are March, April, August and December—also days that add up to **3** and **6** can be of connective importance.

The Three and Four Connective Energy:

Oh boy! What a calamity waiting to happen if they don't know their roles in this relationship. The number **3** person is usually too bubbly, happy and expressive for the number **4's** moodiness and wanting to be to themselves nature. This can be a very stressful union because both have different vibes of expression. You (#3) are a social butterfly (or fire fly) and the 4 person is a weird, structured sort that would probably leave you alone and let you go about your socializing business. If you learn to appreciate the stabilizing attitude of the number 4—this could be a respectable union. The bedroom antics might be different because your flames are fed by the 4's air—but that won't last for long if other parts of your lives don't mesh. No months but if you are trying a little, "Sumthing, Sumthing," days that add up to 3, 4 and 7 might be a choice for you two.

The Three and Five Connective Energy:

This can be a very popular team in many instances. You both are like Peter Pan, "the youth that never grows old"—the number 3 energy is expressive and expansive with the number 5 energy that loves their freedom and has energy to burn. Sexually speaking there isn't anything that can hold you two back— both of you would do it anywhere. (I'm just saying.) The only thing both of you should be concerned with is the emotional and mental nervous tension. This can be a good mix—if it is carefully handled and through meditation, rest and positive affirmations. May, June, October and December are an opportune time for both of you—also days that add up to 3, 5 and 8 are good for some sort of success in your union.

The Three and Six Connective Energy:

Depending on the signs of these two you (3) and the 6 person can be harmony in motion. There is a lot both of you have to offer each other. The both of you enjoy fine art, fine restaurants and overall fine people to hang out with. The expressive, harmonious appreciation for life and its wonders intrigues the both of you. Now, **3** is still a fire number and **6** is an earth number—but this can only compare to the beauty of an out-door barn yard fire and how the flames bounce off of the earth and wood. There might be a little control issue between the **6** and the **3**—but if handled with care and open communication it will have a lasting effect. The months that can help balance it out are March, May, October and December—also days that add up to **3, 6** and **9** are great for any type of advancements.

The Three and Seven Connective Energy:

You love knowledge, wisdom and understanding especially when it comes from someone of interest. That is something that the number **7** person always has to offer because they are the researchers and the philosophers of the bunch. Your outgoing **3** nature can bring many fun times to the **7** person who would rather stay at home and read a good book. Their shy & quiet nature turns you **(#3)** on and it enables you to express yourself to someone who would really listen and give insight to what you may be going through at the time. They **(#7)** enjoy your conversation that can range from sex to science in three breaths without skipping a beat. If both of you can choose a definitive time to go out and enjoy yourselves and then recognize the need to just be home and get into each other's mind, body and soul—this can be a surprisingly good relationship. Yes—even sex will be boiling hot. Your best months together are March, May, and July — also days that add up to **3, 7** and **1** are good for this fire and water union.

The Three and Eight Connective Energy:

The song for this unique bond would be the O'Jay's, *"Money! Money! Money! Money"!* This would be a powerhouse relationship but their roles would have to be defined. You two would make a good couple because number **3** brings the heat of expansion, popularity and creativity to the table—while the number **8** person brings an executive attitude, strength and down-to-earth organizational skills. If you are worried about what could happen during the intimate times—there is no need to concern yourself with that. Just do what you do best and the **8** person will jump to action. The best months to work it out are January, March, May, October and December—also days that add up to **3, 8** and **11** can be of assistance.

The Three and Nine Connective Energy:

This is a match made in *"Elemental Heaven."* But, depending on the signs of these two **(3 & 9)** and their backgrounds it can be something else. Outsiders will watch the flames of this energetic and exhilarating connection of love, art and popularity. There is so much in common with the both of you that it is a shame that the world can't learn to mimic this energy. Your abilities to create an exciting team for business are unmatched in many circles. If both of you decided to make it happen on all levels—the Sun's flames and light would be the only thing that would out shine your accomplishments. Consider the months of March, April, November and December to make your connections —also days that add up to **3** and **9** are good vibratory days for this bond.

The Chronicles of a Number 4 person

If you are born on the 4th, 13th, 22nd or 31st, of any month, you are a number 4 person. This also includes those under the sign of Aquarius.

The Four and One Connective Energy

Air number **4** and Fire number **1** share a planet called the Sun. But there is a sunny side up and sunny side down in this combination. Communication is the key with these elements and depending on the sign it could be a good connection. You **(#4)** need structure and clear communication at all levels or it can get weird. The number **1** person is a leader, *a-go-getter* and a take charge type of person—of which you might be open to. You **(4)** need to get ready before you heat up in any intimate situation and number **1** has to understand that his (or her) *straight-to-the-point* way of doing things is not going to cut it. The months to work your unusual magic are February, June, July and August—also days that add up to **4, 1** and **5** might be helpful in some way.

The Four and Two Connective Energy

Can Structure **(#4)** and sensitive **(#2)** come together? Well, in this case it can, depending on the Zodiac signs they're connected to. Laying a foundation and making plans is something that your number **2** partner will support as long as it makes sense to them. They **(#2)** are very sensitive and intuitive to your needs. Both of you are detail orientated and very thoughtful to each other's desires. The only thing that can hinder this relationship is if you become hateful, insensitive & rough and if your number **2** partner becomes petty, deceptive and insincere. Both of you are emotionally connected and when you bring that connection to the bedroom arena—bubbles are produced from the air and water relations. To make things more lively try February, June, July and August as those months to do it. Also, days that add up to **4, 2** and **6** as a method of achievement can work.

The Four and Three Connective Energy

This is an interesting mix of air and fire—only because the expression is different from say, the **5** and **3** combination. The **4** person is not as outgoing as the **3** person. The number **4** are more in the background and to themselves— Sorry, not the number **3** person; they love an audience and a good party. This can be a more challenging relationship unless you **(#4)** open up and let that communicative, funny and weird side of you free. Now, this can work in the bedroom because both of you are in a private setting and this will allow you both to express yourselves. No months shared but, days that add up to **4, 3** and maybe **7** can bring a connection if your roles are put in perspective.

The Four and Four Connective Energy

You two are one and the same. *(In one sense)* It is almost like looking into a mirror and saying, *"Is that me?"* Both of you are very structured and love organization in the home, at your job, etc. Howsoever, just because you two have the same number doesn't mean that both of you are on same identical road. This weird couple can be extremely opposite and depending on the zodiac it might even bring more unusual energy to the table. You may ask, *"Can it work?"* and I will say, *"Sure it can—but y'all might need some counseling."* In the sack it could be a good match but, at the end of the day, things have to even out for it to work and for a foundation to be laid. You should have a good connection during the months of February, June and August—also days that add up to **4** and **8** like: **13, 17, 22**, etc. will be helpful.

The Four and Five Connective Energy

This is an Air **(#4)** to Air **(#5)** mixture. You are **"the lets**

make plans" type of Air energy and your partner is, **"the any plan is a good plan —let's make it happen"** type of Air energy. Let me school you on how you need to flow with this *"Born free"* character— do not give them restriction, especially if you just started dating. The number **5** will fly like an eagle if you try to put them in a box. Just let them *"be"* and you will keep them for a good while. I will tell you one thing, if you decide to go down the intimate road with them—you better look out because sex is their middle name. Here are some months you should consider linking up with your number **5**—February, June, August and September are great. Also days that add up to **4, 5** and **9** might be good to achieve some air flow.

The Four and Six Connective Energy

This is like *a big wind kicking up dust— and hard to settle.* The elements are not known to work well together but anything can happen. *(Especially if both of you have a compatible sign)* Both of you are known to be trustworthy, loyal and a great service to others. Now, if both of you know where you stand in this relationship it could probably work. However, it might be too much to ask for. The number **6** person can be overly demanding and you may not go for that. Love making between you two will bring about a short sand storm and you don't really have any months in common but, days that add up to **4, 6** and **1** might be of assistance.

The Four and Seven Connective Energy

This is an *"unusually"* good mixture of air and water. *It harmonizes like H2O.* Both of you like to take your time, both are very private and both of you enjoy each other's company. I suggest you two go to parks with a lake or go to places far out but not during tourist season. You do not need to be around a crowd, you two just need the essence of each other. Intimate times will be like a tsunami of love as long as you maintain patience, tolerance and a sincere love for one another. Plan special things in the months of February, July and August—also days that add up to **4, 7** and **2** can be very useful.

The Four and Eight Connective Energy

These numbers are multiples of each other and can work well with each other *depending on the zodiac.* When both of you come together it can be *all heaven or all hell—and if it is good, keep it that way but, if hell shows its ugly head then it is best to leave each other alone.* Long-term companionship is good—if *"fate"* sees it that way. Doing business can be a plus because of the organizational abilities of the **4** person and *the-business-know-how* of the **8** person which can be helpful for a lasting relationship. Your strong attraction can be worth it in the bedroom because of your intense and distinctive air and earth connection. The months that can work for both of you are January, February, July and August —also days that add up to **4, 8** and **3** might be good to achieve your expressive goals.

The Four and Nine Connective Energy

This can be a funny couple. Although Air and Fire can work and does complement each other—however, the **4** person seems to have many people that are secretly scheming against them and the **9** person has those straight up haters. During the private times you both have many past experiences to chat about—some good and some not so well. Both of you may have conflicting ways but, with a little understanding of each other it can possibly work. With your creative and inventive union this can be a very beneficial relationship. Just remember the **9** person loves to make things happen. *They (#9) will "leap and grow their wings on the way down" and you (#4) will ask, "Do you have a parachute for both of us?"* Your intimate encounters will probably be a shocking experience but try to enhance this during days that add up to **4, 9** and maybe **13** as long as you are not afraid of that number. No months but try those days for good results.

The Chronicles of a Number 5 person

If you are born on the 5th, 14th, and 23rd of any month, you are a number 5 person. This also applies to those under the signs of Gemini or Virgo.

The Five and One Connective Energy

These two numbers **(5 & 1)** needs to clarify their position from the start of the relationship. You, number **5,** need your freedom to move and groove the way you want and the **1** person, you choose, can be controlling and very stubborn if you two don't sit down and be straight up with each other in regards to where this union is going. Both of you enjoy your own independence, both love to experience new things and going to new places. Sexual attraction shouldn't be an issue because the number **5** person *"gets-it-in"* without a problem and the **1** person likes the *straight-to-the-point* way of doing it. It is best for both of you to work it out in February, April, June and August and days that add up to **5, 1** and possibly the number **6** should be helpful and balancing.

The Five and Two Connective Energy

These two **(5 & 2)** can be fluid like flowing air over the moving waters in a valley. Because of your somewhat flexible natures this could be a work in progress if both of you understand your position in this union. *(The zodiac can be a factor also)* You, the **5** person is about constant motion and you do not like anyone to dictate your movements with too many inquiries. The number **2** person can adapt but, they will take their time and move accordingly—which you **(#5)** may not be in agreement with and will probably grow impatient. In an intimate setting, this mental air number **(5)** and emotionally persuasive water number **(2)** can produce bubbles of harmony and adaptability with ease. The months to make the connection are May and October—also the days that add up to **5, 2** and maybe **7** will bring some harmony.

The Five and Three Connective Energy

These two youthful numbers **(5 & 3)** are the life of any social outing. They naturally connect on various levels with energy and vitality. They are popular, they love to go to different places and just express their freedoms. This seems like the idea partnership—however, problems can arise if both of you are not patient with each other and more tolerant. Other than that, take pleasure in it while it lasts. In regards to your sexual encounters, there are no problems in that at all. *EXPRESS YOURSELVES!* The best months to get it on—are May and October—also days that add up **5, 3** and possibly **8** can be of successful use.

The Five and Four Connective Energy

Both of you are Air numbers and have different ways of expressing it. You, number **5**, are about quick movement and change and your possible, number **4,** counterpart is about slow movement and building a structured relationship. You **(the 5 person)** know what you want and can attract young and old people to help you move onto the next level. Remember, the **4** person likes to be different and unique in their own way—so if you go one way... then, they are *more-than-likely* to go the other way and this might not work for you in one sense but, you are able to adapt. Tolerance is definitely needed in this union. Sex will be fun & explorative for both of you. Just go with the flow and you will grow. The best months are February, June, August and September—also days that add up to 5, 4 and maybe the number 9 can be lovingly fruitful.

The Five and Five Connective Energy

What an interestingly attractive, outgoing and exciting connection—that can last a long time because of your common goals. You both are travelers, communicators and have quick wit for business and other various fields. Together you are the life of any party and both of you are known as the *jack-of-all-trades*—however, you two have to stay focused and master one thing at a time. Both of you need your own space and should learn to stay away from excessive drinking of alcohol and the use of other substances. There are no problems in the bedroom with you two, just a constant flow of sexual energy. The best times to make this connection are during the months of May, June, September and October also days that add up to **5** and maybe **1** for more creative success.

The Five and Six Connective Energy

This is an interesting combination of change, love and harmony in every way. Both of you are graceful, good looking and add excitement to any gathering. Because of the **6** person's loving nature—people love to be around them, and of course you're the life of the party by nature also number **5**. Just try not to make your number **6** person jealous if you plan on staying with them. Let them know where they stand in the relationship. Love making might take place anywhere—just try not to wake the neighbors! Great months to link with each other are May, June, September and October also days that add up to **5, 6** and **2** might be obliging.

The Five and Seven Connective Energy

These two numbers **(5 & 7)** should have their own separate rooms with a third room for love making— if they ever decided to buy a house. Both are intellectually stimulating to each other and you both enjoy your own space. The only issues that can arise are that the **7** have their moods and has a tendency to shut down when things seem to go wrong. You, on the other hand, love to be out and about. You have to understand when your number **7** partner shuts down; learn to use discretion and other methods of communication to help them avoid depression. This can be a great connection especially during the months of May, June and September— also during days that add up to **5, 7** and **3** could be of assistance.

The Five and Eight Connective Energy

This is more of a business relationship than an intimate one. The **8** person is that executive, *go-get-it*, type of person and you are that adaptable, promoter and enjoyable social butter fly *(or fire fly)*. If you are planning to take the intimate route please take your time and know where each other stands. However, if your *free loving* air number **(5)** can work with the *managerial* earth energy of the **8** person, then they will help you to be stable and show you how to invest your money, time and energy. Now, again, the intimate road might not be beneficial but depending on the zodiac—maybe it can work. No real solid months between you but days that add up to **5, 8** and perhaps **4** can be an eye opener.

The Five and Nine Connective Energy

As a couple **(5 & 9)** your motto should be, *"leap and grow your wings on the way down."* Both of you are risk takers and love the smell of adventure. You both like to *"keep it moving,"* so to speak. You are very supportive of each other and will make a very insightful combination. Together, traveling to distant lands excites you and you both like stimulating things—but try not to overdo it. Numbers **5** and **9** people are prone to addiction and should avoid it at all cost. *Your love making antics can easily start off as a Barn Fire to a rapid Forest Fire—that not even Smokey the Bear could put out.* The best connective months for your fire to blaze are February, April, June and August. Also days that add up to **5** and 9 should be favorable also.

The Chronicles of a Number 6 person

If you are born on the 6th, 15th, and 24th of any month, you are a number 6 person. This also includes those under the sign of Taurus or Libra.

The Six and One Connective Energy

This can be an emotional rollercoaster because of the earth **(6)** and fire **(1)** dynamics. The number **6's** loving and sharing attitude may collide with the **1** person's selfish and arrogant ways—at times. It is not their intentions to be that way but their drive to be the leader can over whelm a relationship.

You are magnetic, sociable and understanding and both of you share a very strong personality. This could work depending on the zodiac. Both of you **(6 & 1)** would have to aid one another with generosity, balance, love and harmony—whether it is in marriage or business. You both would do well as counselors because you both have a great way of giving inspirational advice from two different perspectives. There are no months you share but the suggested days would be those that add up to **6, 1** and probably **7** for a more spiritual base.

The Six and Two Connective Energy

What a good mix of earth **(6)** and water **(2)** this could be. The **6** person is the love seeker and the **2** person is the peace maker—what a match. You, number **6**, can get jealous of the **2** person especially because the opposite sex is drawn to them quite fast. But, if you two are serious this can be a very loving and loyal relationship. The friends you make are long lasting and love to be around the both of you. Your intellectual union would bring about financial success. This can also be a very intimate and unbreakable relationship with understanding and care for each other. The months you share are May, July and October—also the days that add up to **6, 2** and **8** can be helpful in your growth.

The Six and Three Connective Energy

This is a multi-matching couple with many creative possibilities. Their love for beautiful things and places is unmatched when they are together. Both of you **(6 & 3)** love to enjoy yourselves and entertainment of all kinds. Popularity is your middle names and artistic ways of expressing yourselves is your universal game. Together, your magnetic and compelling energies can create a successful business and help maintain a growing relationship— depending on the zodiac. But, you both have to stay focused and avoid jealousy. Communication is the key. The harmonious months are March, May, October and December—also days that add up to **6, 3** and **9** will be helpful in many ways.

The Six and Four Connective Energy

This earth **(6)** and air **(4)** connection is actually somewhat of a—disconnection! Depending on your zodiac signs it could probably work. But, it would need some patience. This can be disastrous. These two elements do not mesh well if there isn't clear understanding of how to deal with each other. Your number **4** partner can be loyal & practical and they have a tendency to be *narrow-minded*, detached and restrictive. You are loving & sociable but can be self-righteous and egotistical. You can try to make it happen but I wouldn't bet on it. There are no mutual months together—but try the days that add up to **6, 4** and maybe **1** for a creative union.

The Six and Five Connective Energy

This could be an unusual love connection if you **(6)** allow the **5** person to be free and be themselves. Both of you are popular and loved by many, but if you plan on locking the **5** person down for too long they will escape and disappear into the sunset. There is a certain flow you two would have to develop in order for this relationship to last. Maybe if you decided to produce something that you both enjoy like: **a weekly entertaining social event that brings you before the people.** That would enhance your relationship—other than that, there would have to be a, *"let them go in order to keep them,"* type of situation and I don't think you can cope with that for too long. You will enjoy their adaptive antics in the bedroom so don't worry about that—just get the other parts of your union together. The months of May, June, September and October are best times to work at it—with days that add up to **6, 5** and **2** for a possible connection.

The Six and Six Connective Energy

This is a commanding set of energy twins. Both earth numbers are driven by love and both are caring humanitarians. They have an attractive blend of cosmic energy that draws people to them. Promoters of education and health can be your strong points if you both strive to be of service to those around you. *"Remember, it is not how much you know that counts—it is how much you care."* You are intimately attracted to each other on all levels and it will be a very sensual experience—to say the least. Your connective months are May, June and October and days that add up to **6, 3** and maybe **9** can bring a universal union.

The Six and Seven Connective Energy

With this earth **(6)** and water **(7)** mixture there is a possible love connection however, you number **6**, would have to deal with their moods swings. Both love education and both are healers in their own way. The **7** person is more to them self and would rather stay at home than go out to a social event. If they do decide to go out... they would probably observe the surrounding and watch you back while you serve your public. At the end of the day you both have to decide if you can work it out and stay together. An intuitive love connection can be achieved if both are on the same page in the moment of intimacy. Try to make the connection in the months of March, May and July or days that add up to **6, 7** and possibly **4** for building your relationship.

The Six and Eight Connective Energy

This is an innovative connection. These two earth numbers can be very helpful to one another. Both of you **(6 & 8)** complement each other with love, support and guidance. Your **(6)** magnetic way of pulling potential business can be very attractive to the number **8** person and they are in awe with your harmonious understanding of art and beautiful things and places. A stable home life is important to both of you and with clear communication and balance this can be a long lasting relationship. Intimate encounters will more than likely be earth shaking and on point. Look for stronger energies of unity during the months of January, May and October—also days that add up to **6, 8** and maybe **5** for an adaptable achievement.

The Six and Nine Connective Energy

What an erotic combination—so to speak. They **(6 & 9)** are the type of couple that would enjoy *make-up-sex*—just because of the nature of these two numbers. The **6** person is full of *earthly love* but can also be *self-righteous* and the **9** person is full of *fiery* love but can be *narrow-minded*. This is also like the mythical stories of the *GOD of Love vs. the God of War*, which is just the same energy on the extreme side of each other. You both have many things in common and would have to put all the cards on the table to figure out how this would work. Traveling to different places would be an added attraction and months like April, May, October and November would be great to do such things. Also, think about days that add up to **6, 9** and **3** for more expansion and improvement.

The Chronicles of a Number 7 person

If you are born on the 7th, 16th, and 25th of any month, you are a number 7 person. This also includes those under the signs of Cancer or Pisces.

The Seven and One Connective Energy

These two **(7 & 1)** really enjoy their privacy and although both are connected to elements that usually don't blend too well—there are exceptions to the rule especially when you know the planets that are linked to the number **7** and the number **1**. The Moon/Neptune **(7)** and Sun **(1)** have an interestingly celestial bond but, can be very independent in their own unique way. Both would have to put their water and fire nature in its proper perspective in order for this to be successful. You **(7)** might have to educate them **(1)** on the benefits of taking their time when it comes to the bedroom and if they are open to it this can be a worthwhile relationship. Take time to bond during the months of February, July and August and choose days that add up to **7, 1** and maybe **8** for perhaps a greater achievement.

The Seven and Two Connective Energy

The Neptune & Moon connection is very intuitive. This union reminds me of a *movie starring Nicholas Cage called, 'NEXT.' In the movie he had telepathic powers and the woman he was waiting for enhanced his abilities 10 folds.* This is a match made in Heaven and both of you seem like you can read each other thoughts. Your masculine energy **(7)** loves its privacy and the natural companionship and feminine energy **(2)** understands every move you make. You are reflections of each other and depending on your zodiac this can be a peaceful and trustworthy union. The months you share are March, May, July and October—also choose days that add up to **7, 2** and maybe **9** for completion.

The Seven and Three Connective Energy

This combination can be an interesting mix if you **(#7)** can deal with the social life of the **3** person. Where you would like to be at home, to yourself, with your books and other tools of research, your **3** counterpart loves the lime light and can be very popular—especially with the opposite sex. However, this is the type of energy that will bring you out of your shell if you will open up that secret part of your heart that needs it. Although, the **3** person can be out there! *So to speak*—their joy for living helps you to overcome your *"worry-wart"* nature. There should be a strong connection in the bedroom but, you **(#7)** like to take your time—and that will be alright with your **3** counterpart. The months like March, May and October are best for you two to work it out. Days that add up to **7, 3** and **1** can help with the creativity.

The Seven and Four Connective Energy

What a workable and lovable blend of energy you two can be—but, both of you just have an unusual way of showing it. On one hand, this can be a very close & private couple and if they can maintain clear communications and overcome each other's moodiness it can work very well. **This also depends on the zodiac.** Your water energy, number **7**, has its own mood swings with a shutdown mechanism and the number **4** person has their mood swings that will make them do things contrary to what is expected. However, with patience & trust this can be a good relationship with astonishing results. The intimate times together will be like *taking a sensual bubble bath with no rush or time constraints.* The months that will arouse this union are February, July and August—and days that add up to **7, 4** and **2** should help this couple.

The Seven and Five Connective Energy

This can be an issue from the gate. You **(7)** might not go for the free-spirited ride that the number **5** person offers. Although, having a little fun can help you in more ways than one—your private life is sometimes more important than the public life and that is what the **5** person enjoys. *Loosen up, number 7 and enjoy life—it is too short not to.* The commonality between you—is that both of you love information and intelligent conversation. Learn to take trips to far places where you both can gain knowledge and don't be afraid to take academic risk—it will be an added plus to this interesting connection of water and air. Choose the months of May, June, July and September for traveling and outings –also days that add up to **7, 5** and **3** should bring some emotional growth and awareness.

The Seven and Six Connective Energy

This could be an intuitively loving relationship if both of you can understand each other's ways. Your **(7)** moods can sometimes drive a person crazy but, if you can learn to relax and enjoy life without allowing external things to worry you—the **6** person can be very helpful with that. The **6** person can bring love, harmony and an earthly balance into your life—if you will receive it. But, if you shut them down and out—then this can be a disaster waiting to happen. This combination will take some serious work on all levels *(Intimately, publicly, etc.)* The months you connect better in are March, May and July—also days that add up to **7, 6** and **4** can be of organizational help.

The Seven and Seven Connective Energy

This double water combination can produce psychic abilities beyond the imagination. Water is your element and this *"nature's blessings"* would help this couple to relax, to see things clearly and dream great things. The *Travelocity Website* should be one of your favorites because you both enjoy exploring different places, preferably, surrounded with water. Where ever you decide to go make sure it is a learning experience to talk about for years to come. Now, with the psychic abilities mentioned earlier, I shouldn't have to say anything about your sexual antics—but, it could be an ***out-of-body*** experience. *(Hint, hint)* Try to seek your connective levels in the months of March, May, July and October and the days that add up to **7** and maybe **2** can be a unify experience also.

The Seven and Eight Connective Energy

The Water **(7)** and Earth **(8)** works in harmony and so can the both of you if you both know your roles in this union. This can be a powerhouse in business especially in property ownership. All you two have to do is plant the seed in fertile soil and it will grow but, if your moodiness **(number 7)** and the number **8's** intolerance gets the best of this relationship then all will turn into mud very quickly. Time is the master key in this relationship and if you both can take time to work out the kinks then this can be very beneficial from the boardroom to the bedroom. Your best months are January and July—also days that add up to **7, 8** and **6** might bring harmony and achievement.

The Seven and Nine Connective Energy

These numbers **(7 & 9)** are a great example of how two different opposing elements can work together with patience, tolerance and respect. Both are highly intuitive and when they unite it is like *steam becoming one with the atmosphere.* You both are knowledge seekers at all levels and meditation should be very helpful for this union because of your need of *spiritual enlightenment.* The only problem that can arise with this couple is that you **(#7)** have a *cold streak* and they **(#9)** have an *emotional streak*—and this can wreak-havoc in this relationship. Be fully open to the universal love of the number **9** and stay focused—it can only make you better in love, sex and business. Look for May and October to be your best months to build in every aspect—also days that add up to **7** and **9** can help.

The Chronicles of a Number 8 person

If you are born on the 8th, 17th, and 26th of any month, you are a number 8 person. This also includes those under the sign of Capricorn.

The Eight and One Connective Energy

These opposing numbers can be a strategic powerhouse in business. Their goal setting mentality can accomplish anything. If both can let your egos go or be put to the side—you two can achieve wonderful things. Your Earth **(8)** energy needs the fire **(1)** energy to blaze the way to success and their fire needs your earth energy to be firm, grounded and secure. Some may consider you both to be heartless but, that is far from the truth. In your private times you can be very sensitive. It is your drive for success that may present this cold, heartless illusion to the world because you both do not like to show weaknesses. In your intimate moments both of you are fully aware of each other's desires and satisfy them accordingly. Look for days that add up to **8, 1** and maybe **9** for that universal connection. Forget about the months—you are better off flowing with the days.

The Eight and Two Connective Energy

This earth **(8)** and water **(2)** combination can become one unit—in the most realistic way ever. The **2** person is a natural supporter of what you want to do and accomplish. Their innate ability to know what you want and need is almost un-heard of and very helpful. Both of you pay close attention to practical things in life and are able to share great accomplishments if you maintain harmony and an honest love for each other. Trust and cooperation is the glue that will keep this union strong. Your intimate times can be very erotic & soothing and I would suggest bathing together as a way of enhancing it. Enjoy each other in the months of January, March, May, July and September and also choose days that add up to **8, 2** and **1** for that creative link.

The Eight and Three Connective Energy

The question is: *can the authoritative and self-reliant **8** (Earth) get along with the creative and popular **3**(Fire)?* Of course they can. As long as each person can work with each other's ways—there will be no issues. Both of you enjoy working and building for the future and both are not afraid to take risk even when the tides are against you—you two keep swimming upstream. The only issues that can come up are…if you, number **8,** become too power-hungry and if your number **3** counterpart becomes vain and self-indulgent. Other than that, this can be a prosperous relationship. **This also depends on the zodiac.** Don't be afraid to express yourself with the number **3** person *(Sexually and other wise)*—they are always ready and willing. The best months for your type of expression are January, March, May, October and December—Also days that add up to **8, 3** and possibly **2** can be of assistance.

The Eight and Four Connective Energy

This is a connection that will have to be seriously considered. Some would say, *"Leave each other alone,"* but, this is a relationship that can last if you play your chips right. Like you **(#8)** your 4 person loves structure and organization and like you, they love hard work as long as there is a goal attached to it. *For example: Michelle (8) and Barack Obama (4) this connection is not coincidental. Money + Structure = Success.* Remember, both numbers have their positions to play and depending on the zodiacs they can maintain a steady growth over the years to come. Sexually, they would enjoy doing it in a secluded park or beach—whatever works! Just try to accomplish this and other things in the months of January, February, July, and August—also try it out on days that add up to **8, 4** and maybe **3** to bring more expression to the union.

The Eight and Five Connective Energy

This can be nerve racking to the **8** person because you believe in controlling what you do and how you do… while, the **5** person can be all over the place without focus. If you do decide to go down this road you **(#8)** can help the number **5** person by teaching them the importance of accomplishing one goal at a time and they **(#5)** can help you with ideas, promotions and attracting more business because that is what they are very good at. Material success would probably stimulate this relationship more—whether in the business world or the world of intimacy. In other words, *making money turns y'all on*. Days that add up to **8, 5** and **4** could help if you two are open and willing to work it out. As far as the months are concerned—Nah!

The Eight and Six Connective Energy

This double earth combination is called, *"Success in Motion."* They share high esteem, responsibility, strong work ethics and so much more, too numerous to mention. These two can accomplish great things as long as they do not get beside themselves and learn to stay harmonious, loving and respectful. Both of you can be loyal and giving—*especially to humanitarian causes*. You both should invest in property because your element is the Earth and that would work wonders for you two. In order for this to really work please avoid intolerance, worry, anxiety and jealousy. This couple is passionate and strong especially during those heated & sexual times. Your best months are January, May and October—also days that add up to **8** and **6.**

The Eight and Seven Connective Energy

These two energies can be very helpful to each other. You **(#8)** need that intuitive nature of the **7** person to think things out and for researching what is needed for any growing family and business. They **(#7)** need your practical attitude and strength to keep them from living in a dream world of worry and to help them avoid nervousness. Take time out for yourselves and learn to appreciate the natural things of life together. Patience and respect is the key to unlock the door to unlimited happiness between you two. The months you share are January and July but days that add up to **8, 7** and **6** can be enjoyable every month.

The Eight and Eight Connective Energy

It's funny, how these two share the same element but can be very hard to get along with if they don't take time to learn each other's strength and learn to compromise when need be. You both are very authoritative and brilliant. Material success can be yours if you both *strengthen your strengths and manage your weaknesses. Watch each other's back!* Set your minds to be supportive of your talents and lay a foundation for both of you and whatever business or family you may establish together. Your intimate encounter will be *down-to-earth* and dirty—so to speak. The months to make it happen are January, March, May, October and December— also choose days that add up to **8** to make things memorable.

The Eight and Nine Connective Energy

This is a good, creative and inventive team with many rewards to gain if both **(8 & 9)** of them respect each other and work hard. Avoid greed, scheming, emotional *out-burst* and *over-indulgence* of any kind and this can work for the long haul. Your **(#8)** thoroughness and controlled attitude will help your number **9** partner release their artistic genius and compassion in more ways than one. This can be a highly powerful & inspirational couple once they undo the knots and learn to work with each other's natural talents. Intimately, both of you are expressive, but it needs a little build up before it takes flight—and you better watch out. To get things moving and working consider January, April, May and October as your worth-while months and also days that add up to **8** and **9** could assist in this connection.

The Chronicles of a Number 9 person

If you are born on the 9th, 18th, and 27th of any month, you are a number 9 person. This also includes those born under the signs of Aries and Scorpio.

The Nine and One Connective Energy

This is one and the same energy that can really blossom into something wonderful with guidance. This combination is full of creativity, originality and will always have fun if they do what they love to do. You **(#9)** are the numerical Omega and they **(#1)** are the numerical Alpha in so many ways. In other words, your number **1** partner will initiate the job and you **(#9)** will definitely finish the job. Together, both are encouraging and exciting to be around. So much heat can be felt from this couple and their energy not only can be seen in love but also in business. **Just learn to understand & respect each other's ways and watch each other's back.** The one thing you will love about each other is that straightforward attitude that you share—this will even be expressed in the bedroom with no limitations. The good months that can assist your blending energies are April and August—also days that add up to **9** and **1** will keep the fire burning.

The Nine and Two Connective Energy

These numbers are usually in opposition to each other in a whole different realm. As you are the humanitarian and the spiritual sort, so is your number **2** counterpart who will always be helpful in any way. They are known as the cooperative number and would love to serve your needs—if you allow them to. However, if you become argumentative and impractical—your mild-mannered number **2** will run for the hills. Other than that, enjoy your gentle and peaceful number **2** partner in every way you can and, for the time you may share. Depending on the zodiac this can go either way—just be understanding and supportive of each other. No monthly connections exist but the most creative days to make this happen would be the days that add up to **9** and **2** of any month.

The Nine and Three Connective Energy

This fire can burn for a long time if these two stay focus, and stay away from over indulgence of any form. Both of you love art of all kinds and enjoy going to events where culture is expressed. The **3** person is very popular and loves the social life and this can be a problem if you don't realize it from early in the relationship. Both of you are confident and very talented and would make a great team. When you two fire numbers are let loose—watch out! You might burn something especially in the love making room. The best months you share are March, April, November and December and days that add up to **9** and **3** should also help.

The Nine and Four Connective Energy

It is said that, *"fire and air are a good mix"* but, in this case you would have to take your time to get to know this number **4** energy to see if they can control their weird tendencies. Now, both of you like things in order but, the **4** person has their own way of putting things in order that may not mesh with your way of doing it. Not saying that it couldn't work—you just have to be sure before you journey into this valley. If you both take the time to understand each other, this could be a well-balanced couple. With your inventive ways of delivering brilliant ideas and their organizational influence and structure—it can be a lasting relationship. Your love life might be as square as the room you're in but, with a fan and some candles this can be a very interesting union. No months but, suggested days that add up to **9** and **4** can be quite appealing.

The Nine and Five Connective Energy

This should be fast, furious and fun. What a combination! — *both are quick-wit*, creative and talented. There will be many adventures with these two but, at the end of day when you **(9)** want to calm the fire and settle down the **5** person might not be around and will keep it moving as usual. No matter how long this relationship last, there will be loads of traveling and learning along the way. At least if you don't remain intimate you can still remain friends and fool around every *now-and-then* if you're not involved with anyone at the time. *It is up to you*. The months you share are April, June and August and days that add up to **9** and **5** are the best times to have your fun.

The Nine and Six Connective Energy

This fire and earth blend has a love for beautiful people, places and things. They can be the best of friends with an unwavering love for each other. The **6** person reminds you that life is about balance and harmony and you **(9)** will remind them that the base of any relationship must be spirituality in order for it to succeed. Support on every level will be the best solution for this combination. Just stay away from petty arguments and jealousy. This is a sexually satisfying connection and it can only get better in time. You are most unifying during the months of April, May, October and November—also days that add up to **9** and **6** are very favorable.

The Nine and Seven Connective Energy

This will be like a psychic affair because of their highly intuitive nature in the fire and water realm. *This is like steam becoming one with its surroundings after the fire and water interaction.* The **7** person is very spiritual—*and you like that.* They would be the one watching your back in the public and vise versa. The only issue here is that the **7** person can be moody if things do not go their way and you will become emotional if you don't understand why they are acting that way. There would have to be a certain understanding and tolerance for you two to keep the love and harmony in this relationship. The months that work for you two, are May and October—also the days that add up to **9** and **7** will work well for your spiritual connection.

The Nine and Eight Connective Energy

This will be an information seeking couple with many things to learn from each other and the world around them. The **8** person is practical and stead-fast with their executive moves and you blend right in. You **(9)** will be the creative fire to bring forth more ideas and business direction. Both are supportive and can galvanize great support from others. This is the numerical meaning of, *"Family is Business and Love is Law."* There is a mutual respect for each other and within time you both will be a shining example to others. During the intimate times you might have to take your time with the **8** person but, when the flames are lit—*it will be worth it.* The months shared are January, April, May and October –also days that add up to **9** and **8** are very useful.

The Nine and Nine Connective Energy

These two fire twins exude *Universal Love, compassion, generosity and artistic genius.* A well-oiled machine in every way—in *love* they can't stop you, and in *business* they can't stop you. *The only people who can deter this complete union—are those involved.* For a couple that seems to have everything going for them the only way this can fall to the wayside is if one of you sabotages it with arrogance, arguments, vulgarity and fickleness. Try to keep busy and always keep your relationship open for growth. Sexually this is a *"no brainer,"* a powerful combination in every way. The favorable months for your continual union are March, April, May, October and December—also days that add up to **9** will bring more FIRE!

REMINDER: THE ASTROLOGICAL CHARTS ARE JUST AS IMPORTANT AS THE NUMERICAL CHARTS—SO, PLEASE STUDY ALL ASPECTS. ALSO, THE PREVIOUS INFORMATION IN THIS BOOK IS ONLY A PART OF THE PUZZLE OF UNDERSTANDING, OVERSTANDING AND INNER-STANDING YOURSELF AND OTHERS. DO NOT LIMIT YOURSELF WHEN IT COMES TO KNOWING WHO YOU ARE. THERE IS MUCH MORE TO LEARN. ☺

Epilogue

"Everybody is a genius, but if you judge a fish by its ability to climb a tree, it will live its whole life believing that it is stupid."
~ Albert Einstein

During my travels and in conversation with various people—the issues I've discovered in my relationships and others have been what each individual has gone through in their past. Whether it involves family, friends, business, etc. it all affects us individually. *I have spoken to many people and I have said that the elements linked to numbers and signs known as **Air, Earth, Fire, Water** and sometimes **Ether** can work together in unison or it can work against us.* Every element has its role in existence. We as humans have to learn how to put these elements in their *perspective places and roles.*

For example, I did a brief reading for a couple a few months ago and their birth dates were:

1st. February 15, 1982
2+1+5+1+9+8+2 = 28 (2+8) = 1

2nd. November 13, 1974
2+1+3+1+9+7+4 = 27 (2+7) = 9

The first person	The second person
Aquarian (Air sign)	**Scorpion (Water Sign)**
6 (Earth personality)	**4 (Air personality)**
1 (Fire Life Path)	**9 (Fire Life Path)**

These two have a very bubbly relationship and when they are in a disagreement it can be very heated or over the top. The **Air sign**
would have to settle the emotions of the **Water sign** or the **Water sign** would have to use the discipline of its **4 personality** and calm the situation down. Also, notice that the **Air sign** has an **Earth personality** that can blend well with the **water sign's** energy and both of them share a similar life path which lets me know that the person with the number **1 life path** has to be first—and that the person with the number **9 life path** has to be accommodating after it is all said and done. That is why we have to learn to put the **signs** and **numbers** in their proper perspective.

Note: For more info, always consult a good astrologist, numerologist or reader.

One of the main reasons why many of us do not get along with each other is because we have chosen to follow the way of life of others who do not respect us and does not wish us any good—because, if they did have our best interest, they would have told us the truth from the beginning and allow us to grow and be the best we deserve to be through our ancient wisdom. Instead they stole what was ancient and available to all and hid it in their *museums, libraries and secret organizations* and use what little they received and controlled the masses.

If we knew that the **science of numbers, astronomy, astrology, solar biology** and other great sciences had been used for **over 10,000 years and more...** we could be a great people beyond what we have become today. Not saying that we are not great! —*I'm just saying we could be Greater.* **Our DNA has the imprint of our ancestors—all we have to do is remember!** We are **all a reflection of the Creator** *(regardless of land, label or language)* and we are all here, on Earth, **having a human experience.** So, remember our ancestors loved us so much that they left us with tools that would assist us back on the path of, **"Know Thy Self."** That is why I decided to place my piece of the puzzle on the board and I hope it will guide you into the overstanding of why— *Numbers 'R' Simple...People are Complicated. Peace, Love and Guidance to All. ~ K. S.* ☺

"Men (and Women) are superior to the stars if he (or she) lives in the power of superior wisdom. Such a person, being master over heaven and earth, by means of his (or her) will, is a magus (or magi), and magic is not sorcery but supreme wisdom" ~ PARACELSUS

Index

A

accident prone, 65
Alchemy, 7
alcohol, 40, 90
Astrology, 6, 7, 8, 9, 21, 49
Astronomy, 6, 7, 21

B

birthday, 16, 17, 18, 48, 49, 51, 67

C

celebrity, 16
Chaldean, 21, 22, 23, 62, 67
child birth, 19
Composite numbers, 37, 38

D

Death Certificate, 4

depression, 55, 63, 91
disomy, 14
Divorce, 4

E

Etymology, 34
Expressive Ego, 59

F

feminine, 11, 12, 13, 15, 16, 18, 32, 49, 97

H

health issues, 5, 62, 63, 64, 65
Health Records, 4
Herbs, 62, 63, 64, 65

J

JUPITER, 26, 27

M

Marriage, 4
MARS, 25, 27
masculine, 11, 12, 13, 15, 16, 18,
32, 97
Master Numbers, 43, 44
MERCURY, 25, 27
MOON, 25, 27
mosaicism, 13

N

non-disjunction, 15
Number, 1, 3, 5, 8, 17, 19, 34, 36,
37, 41, 46, 51, 68, 70, 73, 75, 76,
79, 84, 88, 92, 97, 101, 106

O

out-of-body, 100

P

Partnering Ego, 58
planet, 25, 49, 84

S

SATURN, 26, 27
Self Ego, 56
Solar Numerology, 7, 9, 10, 116
SUN, 25, 27

T

telepathic powers, 97
trisomic, 14

U

universal state, 31

V

Vegetables, 62, 63, 64, 65
VENUS, 26, 27

Recommended Reading

Numbers and You *by Lloyd Strayhorn ~ **1987***

Solar Numerology: *by Nysut: Amun - Re Sen Atum – Re ~ **2013***

Your Days Are Numbered *by Florence Campbell ~ **1931***

Numerology for Healing *by Michael Brill ~ **2009***

Numerology: A Key to Human Behavior *by Harish Johari ~ **1990***

Numerology for Beginners *by Geri Bauer ~ **2000***

Helping Yourself with Numerology *by Helyn Hitchcock ~ **1988***

Book of Numbers *by Cheiro ~ **2012 (Eighth Edition)***

The Compleat Astrologer *by Derek and Julia Parker ~ **1971***

The Story of Paracelus: Magic into Science ~ 1951

A Complete Guide to the Tarot *by Eden Gray* ~ **1970**

How to Win Games of Chance *by Kenneth Dickkerson* ~ **1992**

Resources and How to Contact Us:

For more information, Numerology presentations, lectures, readings and workshops, please contact: 347.496.1022

E-mail: numberrsimple@gmail.com or kingsimonproductions@gmail.com

Charles Child Publishing 440 915-2432

drmelanie16@yahoo.com

16353883R00068

Printed in Great Britain
by Amazon